BITCOIN

Bitcoin:
A Primer for Policymakers

BY JERRY BRITO AND ANDREA CASTILLO

Arlington, Virginia

ABOUT THE MERCATUS CENTER AT GEORGE MASON UNIVERSITY

The Mercatus Center at George Mason University is the world's premier university source for market-oriented ideas—bridging the gap between academic ideas and real-world problems.

A university-based research center, Mercatus advances knowledge about how markets work to improve people's lives by training graduate students, conducting research, and applying economics to offer solutions to society's most pressing problems.

Our mission is to generate knowledge and understanding of the institutions that affect the freedom to prosper and to find sustainable solutions that overcome the barriers preventing individuals from living free, prosperous, and peaceful lives.

Founded in 1980, the Mercatus Center is located on George Mason University's Arlington and Fairfax campuses.

Mercatus Center at George Mason University
3434 Washington Blvd., 4th Floor
Arlington, VA 22201
www.mercatus.org
703-993-4930

Typeset by EEI Communications
Index prepared by Connie Binder

Printed in the United States of America

Library of Congress Cataloging-in-Publication Data

Names: Brito, Jerry, author. | Castillo, Andrea M., author.
Title: Bitcoin : a primer for policymakers / by Jerry Brito and Andrea Castillo.
Description: Arlington, VA : Mercatus Center at George Mason University, [2016] | Includes bibliographical references and index. | Description based on print version record and CIP data provided by publisher; resource not viewed.
Identifiers: LCCN 2016020517 (print) | LCCN 2016017435 (ebook) | ISBN 9781942951179 (Kindle e-book) | ISBN 9781942951162 (pbk.)
Subjects: LCSH: Bitcoin. | Electronic funds transfers. | Money--Law and legislation. | Finance--Law and legislation.
Classification: LCC HG1710 (print) | LCC HG1710 .B75 2016 (ebook) | DDC 332.1/78--dc23
LC record available at https://lccn.loc.gov/2016020517

CONTENTS

"I think that the Internet is going to be one of the major forces for reducing the role of government. The one thing that's missing, but that will soon be developed, is a reliable e-cash, a method whereby on the Internet you can transfer funds from A to B, without A knowing B or B knowing A."

—Milton Friedman, 1999

"The root problem with conventional currency is all the trust that's required to make it work. The central bank must be trusted not to debase the currency, but the history of fiat currencies is full of breaches of that trust. Banks must be trusted to hold our money and transfer it electronically, but they lend it out in waves of credit bubbles with barely a fraction in reserve. We have to trust them with our privacy, trust them not to let identity thieves drain our accounts. Their massive overhead costs make micropayments impossible."

—Satoshi Nakamoto, 2009

"Bitcoin offers a sweeping vista of the opportunity to reimagine how the financial system can and should work in the Internet era, and a catalyst to reshape that system in ways that are more powerful for individuals and businesses alike."

—Marc Andreessen, 2014

I. INTRODUCTION

Bitcoin is the world's first completely decentralized digital currency. Six short years ago, knowledge of it was confined to a handful of hobbyists on Internet forums. Today, the bitcoin economy is larger than the economies of some of the world's smaller nations. The value of a bitcoin (or BTC) has grown and fluctuated greatly, from pennies in its early days to over $1,200 at its peak in November 2013. The current market capitalization of the bitcoin economy is estimated to be roughly $6.4 billion.[1] Businesses big and small have shown an interest in integrating the Bitcoin platform into their operations and in providing new services within the bitcoin economy. Venture capitalists, too, are eager to put their money behind this growing industry.[2] One database of venture capital investments in Bitcoin businesses lists over $1 billion in total known venture capital funding over the past four years, up from $2 million in 2012 to $548 million in 2015.[3] Traditional financial institutions and researchers have also begun to take notice[4]—and to get involved.[5] Noting Bitcoin's rapid development and its status as a "remarkable conceptual and technical achievement," the Federal Reserve Bank of Chicago released a primer on the cryptocurrency in 2013.[6] The development of Bitcoin and its early successes are an exciting testament to the ingenuity of the modern entrepreneur.

Because Bitcoin is decentralized, it can be used pseudonymously, and this has attracted the attention of regulators. The same qualities that make Bitcoin attractive as a payment system could also allow users to evade taxes, launder money, and trade illicit goods. Several federal regulatory bodies, including the Financial Crimes Enforcement Network (FinCEN) of the Department of the Treasury,[7] the Department of Justice,[8] the Internal Revenue Service (IRS),[9] the Commodity Futures Trading Commission (CFTC),[10] the Consumer Financial Protection Bureau (CFPB),[11] the Securities and Exchange Commission (SEC),[12] and the Federal Elections Commission (FEC)[13] have all released official statements regarding the regulation of virtual currencies, including Bitcoin. Some bitcoin financial startups are even currently applying for official registration and oversight from the SEC,[14] while another startup has already sought and secured CFTC approval.[15] States such as New York[16] and California[17] have begun addressing their money-transmission licensing laws in light of virtual currency technologies like Bitcoin. In considering how to best oversee this still nascent technology, government regulators should take care that their overlapping directives do not hinder the promising growth potential of this innovative financial platform.

This primer will provide a short introduction to the Bitcoin network, including its properties, operations, and pseudonymous character. It will describe the benefits of allowing the Bitcoin network to develop and innovate, while highlighting issues of concern for consumers, policymakers, and regulators. It will describe the current regulatory landscape and explore other potential regulations that could be promulgated. It will conclude by providing policy recommendations that will address policymakers' common concerns while allowing for innovation within the Bitcoin network.

II. WHAT IS BITCOIN?

Bitcoin is an open-source, peer-to-peer digital currency. Among the many things that make Bitcoin unique is that it is the world's first completely decentralized digital payments system. This may sound complicated, but the underlying concepts are not difficult to understand.

OVERVIEW

Until Bitcoin's invention in 2008 by the unidentified programmer known as Satoshi Nakamoto, online transactions always required a trusted third-party intermediary. For example, if Alice wanted to send $100 to Bob over the Internet, she would have had to rely on a third-party service like PayPal or MasterCard. Intermediaries like PayPal keep a ledger of account holders' balances. When Alice sends Bob $100, PayPal deducts the amount from her account and adds it to Bob's account.

Without such intermediaries, digital money could be spent twice. Imagine there are no intermediaries with ledgers, and digital cash is simply a computer file, just as digital documents are computer files. Alice could send $100 to Bob by attaching a money file to a message. But just as with email, sending an attachment does not remove it from one's computer. Alice would retain a copy of the money file after she sends it. She could then easily send the *same* $100 to Charlie. In computer science, this is known as the "double-spending" problem,[18] and until Bitcoin, it could only be solved by employing a trusted ledger-keeping third party.

Bitcoin's invention is revolutionary because, for the first time, the double-spending problem can be solved without a third party. Bitcoin does this by distributing the necessary ledger among all the users of the system via a peer-to-peer network. Every transaction that occurs in the bitcoin economy is registered in a publicly distributed ledger, which is called the blockchain. New transactions are checked against the blockchain to ensure that the same bitcoins haven't already been spent, thus eliminating the double-spending problem. The global peer-to-peer network, composed of thousands of users, takes the place of an intermediary; Alice and Bob can transact without PayPal.

One thing to note right away is that transactions on the Bitcoin network are not denominated in dollars or euros or yen as they are on PayPal, but are instead denominated in bitcoins. This makes it a virtual currency in addition to a decentralized payments network. The value of the currency is not derived from gold or government fiat, but from the value that people assign to it. The dollar value of a bitcoin is determined on an open market, just like the exchange rate between different world currencies.

OPERATION

So far we have discussed what Bitcoin is: a decentralized peer-to-peer payments network and a virtual currency that essentially operates as online cash. Now we will take a closer look at how Bitcoin works.

Bitcoin transactions are verified and secured through the clever use of public-key cryptography.[19] Public-key cryptography requires that each user be assigned two "keys," one private key that is kept secret like a password, and one public key that can be shared with the world. The public key is often referred to as a "Bitcoin address."[20] Users can generate as many keypairs as they desire, and they are managed by a Bitcoin "wallet" that acts as a kind of Bitcoin keyring.[21] When Alice decides to transfer bitcoins to Bob, she creates a message, called a transaction, which contains Bob's public key, and she "signs" it with her private key. By looking at Alice's public key, anyone can verify that the transaction was indeed signed with her private key, that it is an authentic exchange, and that Bob is the new owner of the funds. The transaction—and thus the transfer of ownership of the bitcoins—is recorded, time-stamped, and displayed in one "block" of the blockchain. Public-key cryptography ensures that all computers in the network have a constantly updated and *verified* record of all transactions within the Bitcoin network, which prevents double spending and fraud.

What does it mean when we say that the network verifies transactions and reconciles the ledger? And how exactly are new bitcoins created and introduced into the money supply? As we have already seen, because Bitcoin is a peer-to-peer network, there is no central authority charged with either creating currency units or verifying transactions. This network depends on users who provide their computing power to do the logging and reconciling of transactions.

These users are called miners[22] because they are rewarded for their work with newly created bitcoins. Bitcoins are created, or "mined," as thousands of dispersed computers solve complex math problems that verify the transactions in the blockchain. As one commentator has put it,

> The actual mining of bitcoins is by a purely mathematical process. A useful analogy is with the search for prime numbers: it used to be fairly easy to find the small ones (Eratosthenes in Ancient Greece produced the first algorithm for finding them). But as they were found it got harder to find the larger ones. Nowadays researchers use advanced high-performance computers to find them and their achievements are noted by the mathematical community (for example, the University of Tennessee maintains a list of the highest 5,000).
>
> For bitcoins the search is not actually for prime numbers but to find a sequence of data (called a block) that produces a particular pattern when the Bitcoin "hash" algorithm is applied to the data. When a match occurs the miner obtains a bounty of bitcoins (and also a fee if that block was used to certify a transaction). The size of the bounty reduces as bitcoins around the world are mined.
>
> The difficulty of the search is also increased so that it becomes computationally more difficult to find a match. These two effects combine to reduce over time the rate at which bitcoins are produced and mimic the production rate of a

> commodity like gold. At some point new bitcoins will not be produced and the only incentive for miners will be transaction fees.[23]

Thus the Bitcoin protocol was designed so that each miner contributes a computer's processing power toward maintaining the infrastructure needed to support the currency network and verifying transactions in the blockchain. In return, miners are awarded newly created bitcoins. The collective effort of miners' processing power to the network is known as the "hashrate." As more processing power is dedicated to mining and the hashrate increases, the protocol will increase the difficulty of the math problem, ensuring that bitcoins are always mined at a predictable and limited rate. (Conversely, if the network hashrate *decreases*, the protocol will accordingly adjust to *decrease* the difficulty of the math problem, as occurred, for example, in December of 2014.)[24]

This process of mining bitcoins will not continue forever. Bitcoin was designed to mimic the extraction of gold or other precious metals from the earth—only a limited, known number of bitcoins can ever be mined. The arbitrary number chosen to be the cap is 21 million bitcoins. Miners are projected to painstakingly harvest the last "satoshi" (named for the unidentified Satoshi Nakamoto), or 0.00000001 of a bitcoin, in the year 2140. If the total mining power scales to a high enough level, the difficulty in mining bitcoins will have increased so much that procuring this last satoshi will be quite a challenging digital undertaking. Once the last satoshi has been mined, miners who contribute their processing power toward verifying transactions will be rewarded through transaction fees rather than mined bitcoins. This ensures that miners still have an incentive to keep the network running after the last bitcoin is mined.

PSEUDONYMITY

A great deal of the attention given to Bitcoin in the media centers on the anonymity that the digital currency is supposed to lend its users. But this idea stems from a mistaken understanding of the currency.

Because online transactions to date have required a third-party intermediary, they have not been anonymous. PayPal, for example, will have a record of every time Alice has sent Bob money. And because Alice's and Bob's PayPal accounts are tied to their respective bank accounts, their identities are likely known. In contrast, if Alice gives Bob $100 in cash, there is no intermediary and no record of the transaction. And if Alice and Bob don't know each other's identities, we can say the transaction is completely anonymous.

Bitcoin falls somewhere between these two extremes. On the one hand, bitcoins are like cash in that once Alice gives bitcoins to Bob, she no longer has them and Bob does, and there is no third-party intermediary between them who knows their respective identities. On the other hand, unlike cash, the fact that the bitcoin transaction took place between two public keys, the time it took place, the amount of the transaction, and other information is all recorded in the blockchain. Indeed, every transaction that has ever occurred in the history of the bitcoin economy is publicly viewable in the blockchain.[25]

The public keys for all transactions—also known as Bitcoin addresses[26]—are recorded in the blockchain, but they are not tied to anyone's identity. If a person's identity *were* linked to a public key, one could look through the recorded transactions in the blockchain and easily see all the transactions associated with that key. So, while Bitcoin is very similar to cash in that parties can transact without disclosing their identities to a third party or to each other, it is unlike cash in that all the transactions to and from a particular Bitcoin address can be traced. In this way Bitcoin is not anonymous, but pseudonymous.

Tying a real-world identity to a pseudonymous Bitcoin address is not as difficult as some might imagine. For one thing, a person's identity (or at least identifying information, such as an IP address) is often recorded when the person makes a Bitcoin transaction at a website or exchanges dollars for bitcoins at a bitcoin exchange. To increase the chances of remaining pseudonymous, one would have to employ anonymizing software like Tor and take care never to transact with Bitcoin addresses that could be tied back to one's identity.

Finally, it is also possible to glean identities simply by looking at the blockchain. One study found that behavior-based clustering techniques could reveal the identities of 40 percent of the Bitcoin users in their simulated Bitcoin experiment.[27] An early network analysis showed how certain statistical techniques can divulge the financial activity and identities of some Bitcoin users.[28] A later analysis of the statistical properties of the Bitcoin transaction graph garnered similar results with a larger dataset.[29] Another analysis of the same Bitcoin transaction graph reiterated that observers using a special technique called entity merging[30] can observe structural patterns in user behavior and emphasized that this is "one of the most important challenges to Bitcoin anonymity."[31] Indeed, these capabilities are more than theoretical: Ross Ulbricht was found guilty of criminal conspiracies stemming from the operation of the Silk Road online black market in part because prosecutors could trace bitcoins sent from the Silk Road servers directly to Ulbricht's personal wallets.[32]

Recently, two federal agents working on the Silk Road investigation were arrested for allegedly stealing hundreds of thousands of dollars in bitcoins from the black market; they were traced and identified through blockchain analysis.[33] On the other hand, developers regularly propose and test new technological tools that could potentially undermine such blockchain forensic techniques.[34] As in other technological spaces, there is a tension between projects to increase privacy and projects building tools for law enforcement surveillance and consumer transparency. Some developments temporarily increase privacy at the cost of transparency, while others temporarily push law enforcement concerns before privacy. It is unclear which tendency will prevail in the Bitcoin network in the long run.

In general, Bitcoin users do enjoy a much higher level of privacy than do users of traditional digital-transfer services, who must provide detailed personal information to the third-party financial intermediaries that facilitate the exchange.

Although Bitcoin is frequently referred to as an anonymous currency, in reality, it is very difficult to stay anonymous in the Bitcoin network. Pseudonyms tied to transactions recorded in the public ledger can be identified years after an exchange is made. Once Bitcoin intermediaries are fully compliant with the bank-secrecy regulations required of traditional financial intermediaries, anonymity will be even less guaranteed because Bitcoin intermediaries will be required to collect personal data on their customers.

III. BENEFITS

The first question that many people have when they learn about Bitcoin is, "Why would I want to use bitcoins when I can use dollars?" Bitcoin is still a new and fluctuating currency that is not accepted by many merchants, so the uses for Bitcoin may seem mostly experimental. To better understand why people might want to use Bitcoin, it helps to think of it, not necessarily as a replacement for traditional currencies, but rather as a new payment system.

Because there is no third-party intermediary, Bitcoin transactions can be cheaper and quicker than traditional payment networks.[35] And because transactions can be cheaper, and currency units are divisible to the eighth decimal place, Bitcoin can make micropayments and other innovations truly cost-efficient for the first time.[36] Additionally, Bitcoin holds much promise as a way to lower transaction costs for small businesses and global remittances, alleviate global poverty by improving access to capital, protect individuals against capital controls and censorship, ensure financial privacy for oppressed groups, and spur innovation (within and on top of the Bitcoin protocol). On the other hand, Bitcoin's decentralized nature also presents opportunities for crime. The challenge, then, is to develop processes that diminish the opportunities for criminality while maintaining the benefits that Bitcoin can provide.

LOWER TRANSACTION COSTS

First, Bitcoin is attractive to cost-conscious firms looking for ways to lower the cost of doing business. Credit cards have greatly expanded the ease of transacting, but their use comes with considerable costs to merchants. Businesses that wish to offer the option of credit card payments to their customers must first pay for a merchant account with each credit card company. Depending on the terms of agreement with each credit card company, businesses must then pay a variety of authorization fees, transaction fees, statement fees, interchange fees, and customer-service fees, among other charges. These fees quickly add up and significantly increase the cost of doing business. However, if a merchant neglects to accept credit card payments to save on fees, he or she could lose a considerable amount of business from customers who enjoy the ease of credit cards.

Since Bitcoin facilitates direct transactions without a third party, it removes costly charges that accompany credit card transactions. Last year, a high-powered group of investors including Virgin Group's Richard Branson, Yahoo! founder Jerry Yang's AME Cloud Ventures, and the Founders Fund, the venture capital fund headed by Peter Thiel of PayPal and Facebook fame, invested a record-breaking $30 million in the payment-processing company BitPay because of the service's potential to lower the business costs of doing online commerce across borders.[37] The popular wallet and exchange service for consumers, Coinbase, broke that prevailing record for bitcoin startup funding in early 2015, raising $75 million in investments from a group of investors including the Spanish banking consortium BBVA, the New York Stock Exchange, and the famed venture capital firm Andreessen Horowitz, which counts Twitter, Skype, and Facebook as early successes.[38] In fact, small businesses have already started to accept bitcoins as a way to avoid the costs of doing business with credit card companies.[39] Others have adopted the currency for its speed and efficiency in facilitating transactions.[40] Merchants labeled "high risk" by credit card companies may have difficulty finding a payment processor willing to work with them, so they have turned to Bitcoin merchant services providers, like BitPay, as an affordable and convenient alternative to credit card services.[41] Bitcoin could continue to lower transaction costs for businesses that accept it as more people adopt the currency.

Accepting credit card payments also puts businesses on the hook for chargeback fraud. Merchants have long been plagued by fraudulent chargebacks or consumer-initiated payment reversals based on a false claim that a product has not been delivered.[42] Merchants therefore can lose the payment for the item as well as the item itself, and also have to pay a fee for the chargeback. As a nonreversible payment system, Bitcoin eliminates the "friendly fraud" wrought by the misuse of consumer chargebacks, which can be very important for small businesses. As Dan Lee, the manager of a small bodega in Brooklyn, puts it, with Bitcoin "there are lower fees, and you don't have to worry about chargebacks, which is beneficial for merchants. It's better than Visa or MasterCard."[43] These characteristics are so valuable to the business that Lee's Greene Avenue Market offers a 10 percent discount to customers who pay in bitcoins.

Consumers like chargebacks, however, because that system protects them from unscrupulous merchants or merchant errors. Consumers may also enjoy other benefits that merchant-account fees help fund. Indeed, many consumers and merchants will probably stick to traditional credit card services even if bitcoin payments become available. Still, the expanded choices in payment options would benefit people of all preferences.

Those who want the protection and perks of using a credit card can continue to do so, even if they pay a little more. Those who are more price- or privacy-conscious can use bitcoins instead. Not having to pay merchant fees means that merchants who accept Bitcoin have the option of passing the savings on to consumers. In this way, Bitcoin provides more low-cost options to bargain hunters and small businesses without detracting from the traditional credit card services that some consumers prefer.

As an inexpensive funds-transfer system, Bitcoin also holds promise for the future of low-cost remittances. In 2014, immigrants to developed countries sent roughly $427 billion in remittances back to relatives living in developing countries.[44] The amount of remittances is projected to increase to $493 billion by the end of 2017.[45] Most of these remittances are sent using traditional brick-and-mortar wire services such as Western Union and MoneyGram, which charge steep fees for the service and can take several business days to transfer the funds.[46] In the fourth quarter of 2015, the global average fee for sending remittances was 7.37 percent.[47] A report from the Overseas Development Institute finds that "remittance super taxes" on funds sent to Africa—which can exceed 12 percent of the funds transferred—are holding back development in the area.[48] The report recommends that competition and innovation be promoted to improve remittance transfers and aid development. Bitcoin can provide such competition and innovation. Transaction fees on the Bitcoin network tend to be less than 0.0005 BTC, or roughly 1 percent of the transaction.[49] (Of course, third-party bitcoin payment processors would charge a fee on top of this, but it could still be much cheaper than traditional wiring services.) This entrepreneurial opportunity to improve money transfers has attracted investments from big-name venture capitalists.[50] Even MoneyGram and Western Union have contemplated whether to integrate Bitcoin into their business models.[51] Bitcoin allows for fast, inexpensive remittances, and the reduction in the cost of global remittances for consumers could be considerable.

New bitcoin businesses are being formed to specifically facilitate bitcoin remittances from prosperous nations to developing countries.[52] While still an infant industry, the bitcoin remittance space has already bifurcated into specialized market segments to serve the needs of remittance senders on one end and remittance recipients on the other—all while navigating and minimizing the costs incurred by the respective existing legal and regulatory institutions.

To send a bitcoin remittance with fiat currency, a person in the United States or Hong Kong can now employ an "on-ramp" remittance service like Align Commerce[53] or Bitspark,[54] which will transfer the local fiat currency into bitcoins in compliance with the regulations of the prevailing jurisdiction. On-ramp remittance companies can then coordinate with "off-ramp" remittance companies in the recipient country to transfer the bitcoins into the local currency and disburse the funds to the intended recipient. If a remittance sender already has bitcoins, the process is even easier: Simply send the bitcoins to an off-ramp remittance company such as Rebit in the Philippines,[55] ArtaBit in Indonesia,[56] or BitPesa in Kenya.[57] These services allow individuals to enjoy the benefits of lowered costs and shorter delivery times when sending and receiving bitcoin remittances without having to go through the hassle of exchanging bitcoins for fiat currencies by themselves while complying with regulations and securing their own assets.

POTENTIAL TO COMBAT POVERTY AND OPPRESSION

Bitcoin has the potential to improve the quality of life for the world's poorest in other ways, as well. Improving access to basic financial services is a promising antipoverty technique.[58] According to one estimate, 64 percent of people living in developing countries lack access to such services, perhaps because it is too costly for traditional financial institutions to serve poor, rural areas.[59] Because of the impediments to developing traditional branch banking in poor areas, people in developing countries have turned to mobile banking services for their financial needs. The closed-system mobile payment service M-Pesa has been particularly successful in countries such as Kenya, Tanzania, and Afghanistan.[60] Mobile banking services in developing countries can be further augmented by the adoption of Bitcoin.

Other Bitcoin business models seek to streamline bitcoin use in developing economies. For example, LocalBitcoins.com, a listing and escrow service for individual small bitcoin traders, publicizes trader information in over 190 countries, including Bangladesh, Zimbabwe, the Democratic Republic of the Congo, Pakistan, Venezuela, Romania, India, and Libya.[61]

Charities in the United States have also looked to Bitcoin as a promising way to alleviate poverty. Bitcoin's ease and affordability for transferring funds makes it an attractive option to lower operation costs for cash-strapped charities. The Bitcoin100 charity campaign has donated bitcoins to a number of causes since 2011.[62] Sean's Outpost, a homeless-outreach organization located in Pensacola, Florida, has been providing meals and toiletries to Pensacola's neediest solely with bitcoins.[63] The charity's founder, Jason King, has opened a nine-acre homeless sanctuary, fittingly titled Satoshi Forest, which is paid for entirely with donations of bitcoins.[64] According to King, Bitcoin's low costs and ease of transfer make it an ideal currency for his charity. "Anyone being able to send money to us in the world instantaneously is very valuable, and we've gotten donations from over twenty-three different countries," he explains.[65] As an open-system payment service, Bitcoin can provide low-income people in developing and developed countries alike with inexpensive access to financial services on a global scale.

Bitcoin might also provide relief to people living in countries with strict capital controls because the total number of bitcoins that can be mined is capped and cannot be manipulated. Furthermore, there is no central authority that can reverse transactions or prevent the exchange of bitcoins between countries. Bitcoin therefore provides an escape hatch for people who desire an alternative to their country's devalued currencies or frozen capital markets. We have already seen examples of people turning to Bitcoin to evade the harmful effects of capital controls and central-bank mismanagement. Some Argentines, for instance, have adopted Bitcoin in response to the country's dual burdens of a 25 percent inflation rate and strict capital controls.[66] Consumer confidence, too, continues to plunge in Argentina.[67] Demand for bitcoins is so strong there that one popular bitcoin exchange is planning to open an Argentine office.[68] Argentine bitcoin use continues to surge in the face of Argentina's capital mismanagement.[69] For example, the Net Party, an Argentine political reform movement, was funded almost entirely with donations in bitcoins. "There you can see the difference: the speed of money," says founder Santiago Siri. "[Raising] the money would have taken eight weeks [using the official currency]; it took one hour with Bitcoin."[70]

Individuals in oppressive or emergency situations might also benefit from the financial privacy that Bitcoin can provide. There are many reasons why people seek privacy in their financial transactions. Spouses fleeing abusive partners need some way to discreetly spend money without being tracked. People seeking controversial health services desire financial privacy from family members, employers, and others who might judge their decisions. Recent experiences with despotic governments suggest that oppressed citizens would benefit greatly from the ability to make private transactions free from the grabbing hands of tyrants. Bitcoin provides some of the privacy that has traditionally been afforded through cash—with the added convenience of digital transfer.

STIMULUS FOR FINANCIAL AND TECHNOLOGICAL INNOVATION

One of the most promising applications of Bitcoin is as a platform for innovation. The Bitcoin protocol contains the digital blueprints for a number of useful financial and legal services that programmers can easily develop. Since bitcoins are, at their core, simply packets of data, they can be used to transfer not only currencies but also stocks, bets, and sensitive information.[71] Some of the features that are built into the Bitcoin protocol include micropayments, dispute mediations, assurance contracts, and smart property; the last allows individuals to control ownership of an item through agreements made in the Bitcoin blockchain.[72] A related concept, smart contracts, allows individuals to automate contracts using the Bitcoin protocol to exchange ownership of a good or service once a condition is met.[73] These features would allow for the eventual development of Internet translation services, instantaneous processing for small transactions (like automatically metering Wi-Fi access), Kickstarter-like crowdfunding services, and even distributed mesh networking, which would allow computers and devices to connect directly to each other instead of being connected by a third party Internet service provider or phone company.

Indeed, early initiatives have already materialized. The crowdfunding platform Pozible began allowing project creators to amass microdonations in bitcoins for minuscule transaction fees in 2013.[74] Decentralized platforms like Swarm utilize blockchain technology to match creators and funders to produce crowdfunded projects.[75] The open-source project Lighthouse is a similar venture that specifically aims to crowdfund bounties for developers of Bitcoin Core (the original Bitcoin client that serves as the backbone of the entire network) to improve the software, but these bounties can be used to crowdfund any project, including charitable causes.[76] There have already been successful Lighthouse-powered decentralized crowdfunds for purchasing medical equipment for charities[77] and for the GnuPG email encryption software.[78] The BitHub platform, too, started allowing software and technology developers of any project to receive micropayments for completed code in 2013.[79] The open-source payment platform Bitmonet provides Internet content creators with a way to monetize their blogs or portfolios using bitcoins.[80] As the bitcoin economy further matures, such innovative applications will continue to materialize.

Bitcoin likewise has catalyzed more complex orders of financial innovation.[81] Professional bitcoin derivatives exchanges have recently started or finalized the process of applying for and receiving official regulatory licensing and oversight. These exchanges include TeraExchange and LedgerX. At the same time, an underground ecosystem of bitcoin-based derivatives exchanges, stock markets, and other information markets has been experimenting with innovative, if legally questionable, financial arrangements for about as long as Bitcoin has been in existence. Unwilling or unable to submit to established regulatory processes, a number of ventures, such as ICBIT Trading, MPEx (which also serves as a bitcoin-based securities market), and Magnr (formerly BTC.sx) have for years been offering bitcoin derivatives that are bought and sold, not for dollars or any other fiat currency, but for bitcoins.

There are also sites online that essentially serve as exchanges for shares of stock denominated in bitcoin. A small number of entrepreneurs have turned to these exchanges to raise capital and sell stock in their companies for bitcoins. The companies and funds listed on these exchanges tend to be bitcoin-related businesses, such as manufacturers of mining equipment, but they have also included bitcoin-denominated gambling sites like Satoshi Dice and BitBet. Because they operate in a kind of digital Wild West, bitcoin securities markets have sometimes been plagued by frauds and scams with little recourse for investors. This was the case with the Bitcoin Savings and Trust (BTCST) fund listed on the defunct Global Bitcoin Stock Exchange (GLBSE). BTCST was eventually ruled to have been a Ponzi scheme in a federal lawsuit filed by the SEC.[82] Alternatively, platforms like the MPEx stock exchange actively discourage novices from trading through a complicated user interface, and they promote transparency through periodic shareholder reports. Whether purportedly self-regulating or not, bitcoin-based derivatives and stock markets will continue to face regulatory scrutiny from bodies that hold the appropriate jurisdiction, as we will discuss later.

Developers and entrepreneurs have also experimented with using Bitcoin technology to facilitate information and prediction markets. Prediction markets can take the form of simple gambling—such as guessing whether or not a random number generator will make one a winner on bitcoin-denominated gambling sites like BitBet.[83] More complex and socially useful prediction markets allow individuals to make bets on the outcomes they think most likely for future events in politics, business, sports, and culture. By allowing individuals to "put their bitcoins where their mouths are," prediction markets can generate valuable insights about the likelihoods of events by better incentivizing individuals to share and value relevant information.[84] One successful example of a popular non-Bitcoin prediction market was Intrade, which facilitated predictions about US election results that were often more accurate than media pundits with a supposed expertise in political projections.[85] Intrade stopped operations in the United States after the CFTC sued the service for illegally selling futures contracts.[86] But prediction markets were revived through Bitcoin technology with platforms like Predictious.com, BTCOracle, and Bets of Bitcoin. The Augur prediction market built on the Ethereum platform is slated to launch in the Spring of 2016.[87] Pure information markets that allow individuals to buy and sell valuable information—like a whistleblower leak of government or corporate corruption—are also operating using Bitcoin technology.[88]

Bitcoin's core innovation is the blockchain ledger technology that allows information to be coordinated, verified, and recorded in a distributed manner. Once this innovation was revealed publicly, anyone could employ the concept in their own digital currency. Enterprising programmers and entrepreneurs have tweaked or simply duplicated Bitcoin's consensus-reaching method and have applied it in novel ways. A constellation of alternative coins, or "altcoins," has since proliferated in the wake of Bitcoin's genesis.[89]

One of the most popular altcoins, Litecoin, is nearly identical to the Bitcoin system but with important differences. The designer wanted to create an alternative coin whose mining process did not result in the kind of hardware arms race that Bitcoin was experiencing;[90] he therefore employed the novel "scrypt" mining algorithm as its consensus mechanism rather than Bitcoin's SHA-256.[91] The Zcash project seeks to engineer a new cryptocurrency that provides the same functionality as Bitcoin along with enhanced privacy and fungibility.[92] Even Internet jokes can make a splash in the cryptocurrency world. The popular "Doge" meme of a Shibu Inu dog gazing mischievously at the viewer surrounded by ungrammatical phrases was memorialized as a joke in the Dogecoin cryptocurrency. As a result, Dogecoin notably enjoyed flurries of market activity,[93] a passionate following, and even NASCAR sponsorship.[94] Hundreds of these altcoins have been launched since Bitcoin started gaining popularity five years ago, but only a few dozen cryptocurrencies have market capitalizations of over one million at any given time. Because of its first-mover advantage, Bitcoin enjoys much greater network effects than any other cryptocurrency, and by almost any measure—market capitalization, number of users, number of transactions, network computing capacity, etc.—it is orders of magnitude larger than its closest competitors.

Programmers can also develop alternative protocols to complement or run directly on top of the Bitcoin protocol in the same way that the Web and email are run on top of the Internet's TCP/IP protocol. Many projects seek to develop software that will interface directly with the Bitcoin protocol. For example, the Colored Coins project seeks to develop a software layer on top of the Bitcoin protocol that would allow users to "color" specific bitcoins and to represent real-world assets like gold, property, or commodities that could then be traded using the network.[95] In 2015, Nasdaq announced that it was planning on integrating colored coin functionality to allow users to issue and transfer securities on the Bitcoin blockchain.[96] By late 2015, Nasdaq's private markets blockchain project, Linq, was being tested by six startups and investors as means of managing asset trading and ownership.[97] Another programmer created a digital notary service to anonymously and securely store a "proof of existence" for private documents on top of the Bitcoin protocol.[98] The Open Transactions platform, which predates the Bitcoin protocol, employs Chaumian untraceable cash techniques[99] and a system of federated servers to improve the privacy and security of digital currency transactions without requiring any changes to the Bitcoin protocol.[100]

Other projects try a related but distinct approach to blockchain innovation. Rather than developing software to interact with and enhance the Bitcoin network, these programmers create new blockchains to power their own desired noncurrency concepts. For example, the Bitmessage team has adopted the Bitcoin model as a way to encrypt digital communications.[101] Namecoin, the first "fork," or derivative copy, of the Bitcoin software, is a distributed, open-source information registration system based on blockchain technology that could theoretically serve as a decentralized replacement[102] for the hierarchical Domain Name System (DNS) that currently serves as the Internet's primary directory service.[103] The new Foxtrot initiative from payment processor BitPay is intended to create a decentralized mesh network using blockchain methods.[104]

Still others seek to employ blockchain technology to distribute computing generally. A helpful metaphor for understanding such projects is the development of cloud computing. For decades, we ran most applications on our desktop computers. More complex functions might be processed by physical servers within the user's vicinity. But for most computer users, all of their important data was contained on their personal hard drives, and the applications that one used to access that data ran locally on one's computer. Should anything have happened to our hard drives, all of our data would be lost unless we had the foresight to frequently back it up. The advent of cloud computing changed all of this. Today, our applications and data are increasingly moving to the cloud. Instead of Microsoft Word running locally on one's computer, one might use Google Docs running in a web browser. Instead of storing family photos in one's hard drive, one might instead use Flickr or Facebook to keep and share photos.

Projects like Ethereum[105] and MaidSafe[106] aim to extend the logic of cloud computing to distributed systems. Instead of relying on HP or Amazon or Microsoft to maintain cloud servers, blockchain technology could provide similar functions with distributed computing. These developers envision a future where cryptography and distributed consensus mechanisms form platforms on which entrepreneurs and programmers can experiment with new applications, currencies, and business models at low cost and with few vulnerabilities to "trusted" third parties. This means that cloud applications will still run in the cloud, just as YouTube or Google Docs do today, but instead of "the cloud" being a metaphor for Google-run servers, it would become truly nebulous, running on the shared resources of thousands of distributed computers and not controlled by any central authority.

Given this impressive array of projects spurred or augmented by the initial Bitcoin blockchain, we are often asked why the title of this booklet is *Bitcoin: A Primer for Policymakers* rather than speaking broadly of cryptocurrencies or listing other popular coins. Our reason is simple: Bitcoin was the first cryptocurrency, so it enjoys beneficial network effects that help it to, by and large, dominate the space. Bitcoin leads in any metric we could choose. On a psychological level, Bitcoin serves as a foundational technology because it is the digital currency that first introduced the blockchain innovation. The romantic genesis story of a pseudonymous programmer secretly toiling to bring light to the world and an exit from the global financial system imbues Bitcoin with added emotional appeal. At the time of this writing, Bitcoin's market capitalization of roughly $6.4 billion exceeds the closest competitor, Ethereum, by 7 times, and the third contender, Ripple, by 25 times.[107] Venture capital investments in Bitcoin companies also outpace the others and are on track to exceed $1 billion since 2012 in 2015.[108] Likewise, Bitcoin by far dominates other cryptocurrencies in the total number of users,[109] network nodes,[110] active addresses,[111] average number and value of transactions per hour,[112] and number of accepting merchants.[113]

In fact, the network effect enjoyed by Bitcoin presents an unfortunate barrier to cryptocurrency innovation. The Bitcoin protocol lacks many experimental features that competing coins seek to provide, but Bitcoin developers are necessarily conservative in the changes that they will integrate to the core protocol. The "sidechains" development project, led by cryptocurrency pioneer Adam Back, seeks to change the core Bitcoin protocol to allow bitcoins to be transferred between the Bitcoin blockchain and a potentially infinite number of "pegged sidechains" that are "sharded" from the primary blockchain.[114] In other words, alternate cryptocurrencies could be programmed into new blockchains that are pegged to an initial amount of bitcoins and convertible with the original Bitcoin blockchain. Since sidechain tokens would be tied to the existing liquidity and value of the Bitcoin blockchain, developers and entrepreneurs would be better able to experiment with new features while facing fewer barriers to adoption and more opportunities to compete in the market. If implemented, sidechains could render Bitcoin a kind of "reserve currency of the entire cryptocurrency sector."[115]

Regardless of whether any particular venture succeeds or fails, it is remarkable that the Bitcoin protocol provides opportunities for programmers and entrepreneurs to experiment with such a diverse range of useful applications. Bitcoin is thus the foundation upon which other layers of functionality can be built. The Bitcoin project can be best thought of as a process of financial and communicative experimentation. Policymakers should take care that their directives do not quash the many promising innovations developing within and on top of this fledgling protocol.

IV. CHALLENGES

Despite the benefits that it presents, Bitcoin has some downsides for potential users to consider. It has exhibited considerable price volatility throughout its existence. New users are at risk of improperly securing or even accidentally deleting their bitcoins if they are not cautious. Additionally, there are concerns about whether hacking could compromise the bitcoin economy.

VOLATILITY

Bitcoin has weathered at least six significant price adjustments since 2011.[116] These adjustments resemble traditional speculative bubbles: overoptimistic media coverage of Bitcoin prompts waves of novice investors to pump up bitcoin prices.[117] The exuberance reaches a tipping point, and the value eventually plummets. Newcomer investors eager to participate run the risk of overvaluing the currency and losing their money in a crash. Bitcoin's fluctuating value makes many observers skeptical of the currency's future.

Does this volatility foretell the end of Bitcoin? Some commentators believe so.[118] Others suggest that these fluctuations are stress testing the currency and might eventually decrease in frequency as mechanisms, such as derivatives markets,[119] develop to counteract volatility.[120] The handful of unregulated bitcoin derivatives markets that had partially filled this need in the early days, like MPEx and ICBIT Trading, are now giving way to professional, regulated bitcoin derivatives and swaps markets. The first US-regulated bitcoin swaps exchange, TeraExchange, began operations under CFTC supervision in September of 2014.[121] Another startup, LedgerX, submitted an application to the CFTC for registration as a bitcoin derivatives clearing organization and bitcoin swap execution facility in December of 2014. CFTC is currently reviewing the application[122] but granted LedgerX temporary registration in September of 2015.[123] Other professional ventures include Crypto Facilities in the United Kingdom[124] and BitMEX in Hong Kong.[125]

It is possible that the price of bitcoins will become less volatile as these derivatives markets continue to develop and as more people become familiar with the Bitcoin technology and develop realistic expectations about its future. Indeed, some measures of historical bitcoin volatility suggest that volatility has already been trending downward over time, as figure 1 displays.

Even if bitcoin volatility reversed course and became more of a problem, it would not imperil all possible uses of Bitcoin. If bitcoins were only used as stores of value or units of account, the currency's volatility could indeed endanger its future: It does not make sense to manage business finances or keep savings in bitcoins if the market price swings wildly and unpredictably. When Bitcoin is used as a medium of exchange, however, volatility is less of a problem.[126] Merchants can price their wares in terms

Figure 1. Historical Bitcoin Volatility, August 2010–August 2015

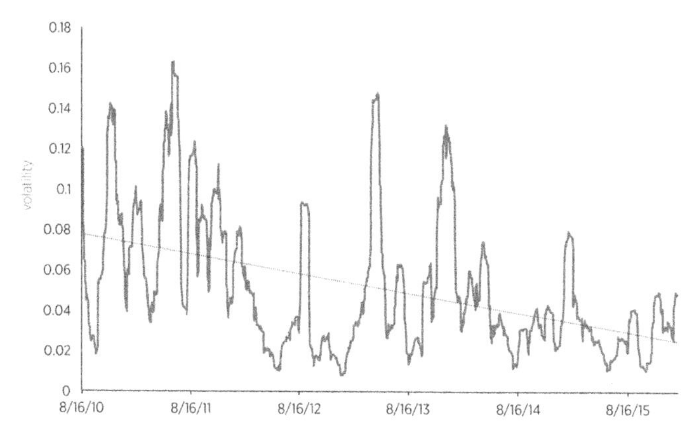

Source: btcvol.info index of CoinDesk data, Eli Dourado, accessed February 1, 2016.
Note: Volatility is measured as the standard deviation of daily returns for the preceding 30-day window. Dotted line represents linear trend line. Produced by Andrea Castillo, Mercatus Center at George Mason University, 2016.

of a traditional currency and accept the equivalent number of bitcoins. Customers who purchase bitcoins to make a one-time purchase don't care about what the exchange rate will look like tomorrow; they simply care that Bitcoin can lower transaction costs in the present. Bitcoin's usefulness as a medium of exchange might explain why the currency has grown more popular among merchants in spite of price volatility.[127]

SECURITY BREACHES

As a digital currency, Bitcoin presents some specific security challenges. However, it is important to distinguish the security outlook for "Bitcoin" the protocol from "bitcoins" the currency units that are secured using wallet software. The Bitcoin *protocol* is virtually unhackable.[128] In contrast, wallet software storing bitcoin *currency units* can be hacked but only to the same extent that one's traditional bank account can be hacked through poor password or security management on the part of the account holder or financial institution—as was the case, for example, with last year's hack of Home Depot that resulted in billions in fraudulent charges.[129]

The Bitcoin protocol is among the most secure technologies in operation today because it integrates two well-known and widely vetted cryptographic tools into its core structure for which no attacks or breaks are known to date. On a micro level, the protocol ensures the security of transactions sent among different wallets by requiring senders to "sign" a transaction with a private key generated by the trusted elliptic curve digital signature algorithm (ECDSA).[130] On a macro level, the protocol ensures blockchain security through the hashcash proof-of-work mining function based on the trusted SHA-256 algorithm.[131] So long as these prevailing cryptographic methods remain secure and impervious to hacking attempts, the Bitcoin protocol should continue to likewise be impervious to malicious attack.[132] Indeed, computer security researcher Dan Kaminski was unable to hack the Bitcoin protocol after several attempts despite his broad knowledge of system vulnerabilities and breach methods.[133]

However, this does not imply that bitcoins as currency units stored in wallets are equally secure. As the information security joke goes, the security risks surrounding bitcoins as currency exist between chair and keyboard. If people are not careful, they can inadvertently delete or misplace their Bitcoin passwords known as private keys. Once that data is lost, the money is lost, just as with paper cash. If people do not protect their private Bitcoin keys, they can leave themselves open to theft.

Bitcoin wallets can now be protected by encryption, but users must choose to activate the encryption. If a user does not encrypt his or her wallet, bitcoins could be stolen through malware.[134]

Bitcoin exchanges, too, have at times struggled with security. In many cases, exchanges have responded to incidents responsibly. Different hackers have successfully stolen 24,000 BTC ($250,000) from a bitcoin exchange called Bitfloor in 2012,[135] siphoned 19,000 BTC ($5 million) from the popular Bitstamp exchange in January of 2015,[136] and another 150 BTC ($41,300) from Coinapult, one of the longest-operating Bitcoin startups, in March of 2015.[137] In each case, the exchange operators repaid or committed to repay the full value of customers' accounts. Another noteworthy incident was the 267 BTC ($934,000) extraction from the widely trusted Blockchain.info service in December of 2014, which was later revealed to have been orchestrated by a Good Samaritan or white hat hacker intending to expose security vulnerabilities in the service.[138] The hacker, "johoe," returned all of the stolen bitcoins upon proof of ownership.[139] Needless to say, the embarrassment caused by this stunt prompted Blockchain.info to quickly and robustly strengthen its internal security.[140]

But other bitcoin exchanges have unfortunately proven to be unscrupulous and even fraudulent. The case of Mt. Gox provides an especially dramatic cautionary tale. As the first functional bitcoin exchange, Mt. Gox enjoyed broad name recognition, and by 2013 it came to manage around 70 percent of all Bitcoin transactions.[141] But volume of business did not translate into duty of care: By November of 2013, customers reported that their requests to withdraw funds from their accounts had been delayed by days or even months.[142] Rumors swirled for months with no official statements from Mt. Gox. In February of 2014, the exchange suddenly filed for bankruptcy in Japan, revealing that it had lost an astounding 850,000 BTC ($473 million) in a suspected hack.[143] However, one analysis of the forensic evidence disputes the official Mt. Gox story, suggesting that trading patterns indicate that a Mt. Gox employee, not an external hacker, absconded with the bitcoins.[144] Mt. Gox customers still had not been reimbursed by the end of 2014,[145] although customers were at least permitted to file claims for lost bitcoins by April of 2015.[146]

Bitcoin services eager to demonstrate their accountability and trustworthiness to their customers have started to take proactive measures to verify their system integrity. Companies like Coinbase[147] and BitGo[148] now prominently publicize their account security insurance policies to prospective customers. Bitcoin exchanges such as Kraken[149] have undergone third-party audits of its bitcoin reserves to try to prove that they can cover their customers' balances. Market competition and legal liability should continue to weed out unscrupulous actors from bitcoin service providers and improve the general security practices of third-party platforms.

Of course, many of the security risks facing Bitcoin are similar to those facing traditional currencies. Dollar bills can be destroyed or lost, personal financial information can be stolen and used by criminals, and banks can be robbed or targeted by distributed denial of service (DDoS) attacks, where malicious actors attack websites with massive amounts of Internet traffic. Bitcoin users should take care to learn about and prepare for security concerns just as they currently do for other financial activities.

CRIMINAL USES

There are also reasons for policymakers to be apprehensive about some of Bitcoin's applications. Because Bitcoin is pseudonymous, policymakers and journalists have questioned whether criminals can use it to launder money and accept payment for illicit goods and services. Indeed, like cash, it can be used for ill as well as for good.

For one example, we can look at the shuttered Deep Web[150] black market site known as Silk Road. While in operation from February 2011 to October 2013, Silk Road took advantage of the anonymizing network Tor and the pseudonymous nature of Bitcoin to make available a vast digital marketplace where one could mail-order drugs and other licit and illicit wares. Although Silk Road administrators did not allow the exchange of any goods that resulted from fraud or harm, like stolen credit card information or photographs of child exploitation, it did allow merchants to sell illegal products like forged identity documents and illicit drugs. The pseudonymous nature of Bitcoin allowed buyers to purchase illegal goods online in the same way that cash has been traditionally used to facilitate illicit purchases in person. One study estimated that total monthly Silk Road transactions amounted to approximately $1.2 million.[151] But the bitcoin market amassed $770 million in transactions during June 2013; Silk Road sales constituted a small drop in the total bitcoin economy bucket.[152]

Bitcoin's association with Silk Road has tarnished its reputation. Following the publication of an article on Silk Road in 2011,[153] senators Charles Schumer and Joe Manchin sent a letter to Attorney General Eric Holder and the Drug Enforcement Administration's administrator, Michele Leonhart, calling for a crackdown on Silk Road, the anonymizing software Tor, and Bitcoin.[154] Their concerns were later addressed. Following a two-year investigation into the Deep Web market, the FBI shut down the Silk Road website on October 2, 2013, and arrested Ross Ulbricht, the man alleged to be its infamous operator known only as the Dread Pirate Roberts.[155] The FBI confiscated all bitcoins associated with Silk Road in a seizure totaling an unprecedented 26,000 BTC, worth $3.6 million at the time of the transfer.[156] Many of the largest merchants on Silk Road, too, have been indicted since Silk Road's closure.[157]

The end of Silk Road has not eliminated the problem of illicit trade. Other Deep Web black markets, such as Black Market Reloaded,[158] Sheep Marketplace,[159] and the relaunched Silk Road 2.0,[160] presented new challenges for law enforcement after the original Silk Road was shut down. One investigation estimates that as many as 43 Deep Web black markets opened up in 2014 alone.[161] However, some of these alternatives have been short-lived: At least 46 markets closed during 2014. Sheep Marketplace went offline permanently in late November 2013 following an exploited vulnerability that cost customers $6 million; Black Market Reloaded voluntarily shut down shortly thereafter in response to security concerns;[162] and Silk Road 2.0 succumbed to the fate of its predecessor and was seized by US authorities and shut down in November of 2014.[163] Today, roughly 30 Deep Web markets are known to be in varying states of operation,[164] although these markets are finding it more difficult to establish the trust and customer base necessary for profitable operation with each law enforcement bust or internal collapse of a large market. For this reason, groups of developers have started experimenting with distributed Deep Web market platforms that theoretically cannot be shut down by targeting any one server or operator.[165]

Another concern policymakers have is that Bitcoin can be used to launder money and to finance terrorism. Although these worries are currently more theoretical than evidential, Bitcoin could indeed be an option for those who wish to discreetly move ill-gotten money. Concerns about Bitcoin's potential to facilitate money laundering were stoked after Liberty Reserve, a private, centralized digital currency service based in Costa Rica, was shut down by authorities on charges of money laundering.[166]

While Liberty Reserve and Bitcoin appear similar because they both provide digital currencies, there are important differences between the two. Liberty Reserve was a centralized currency service created and owned by a private company, allegedly for the express purpose of facilitating money laundering. Bitcoin is not. The transactions within the Liberty Reserve economy were not transparent. Indeed, Liberty Reserve promised its customers anonymity. Bitcoin, on the other hand, is a decentralized open currency that provides a public record of all transactions. Money launderers may attempt to protect their Bitcoin addresses and identities, but their transaction records will always be public and accessible at any time by law enforcement. Laundering money through Bitcoin, then, can be seen as a much riskier undertaking than using a centralized system like Liberty Reserve. Additionally, several bitcoin exchanges have taken steps to comply with anti–money laundering (AML) record-keeping and reporting requirements.[167] The combination of a public ledger system and the cooperation of bitcoin exchanges in collecting information on their customers will likely make Bitcoin less attractive to launderers relative to private anonymous virtual currencies.

It is also important to note that many of the potential downsides of Bitcoin are the same as those facing traditional cash. Cash has historically been the vehicle of choice for drug traffickers and money launderers, but most US policymakers would never seriously consider banning cash. As regulators begin to contemplate Bitcoin, they should be wary of the perils of overregulation. In the worst-case scenario, regulators could prevent legitimate businesses from benefiting from the Bitcoin network without preventing money launderers and drug traffickers from using bitcoins. If bitcoin exchanges are overburdened by regulation and shut down, for instance, money launderers and drug traffickers could still put money into the network by paying a person in cash to transfer his or her bitcoins into their virtual wallets. In this scenario, beneficial transactions are prevented by overregulation while the targeted activities are still able to continue. The challenge for policymakers and regulators is how to develop a system of oversight that assuages their twin concerns about money laundering and illicit purchases without smothering the benefits that Bitcoin is poised to provide to legitimate users in their everyday lives.

V. REGULATION

Current law and regulation does not cover a technology like Bitcoin, so it has existed in something of a legal gray area. Bitcoin does not exactly fit existing statutory definitions of currency or other financial instruments or institutions, making it difficult to know which laws apply and how.

This situation is reminiscent of regulatory uncertainty surrounding other new technologies such as Voice over Internet Protocol (VoIP).[168] When VoIP first emerged, the Communications Act and Federal Communications Commission (FCC) regulations only covered voice communications over the traditional public switched telephone network. Like Bitcoin, VoIP competed with a highly regulated legacy network, was less expensive, and was often peer-to-peer. To this day, Congress and the FCC continue to grapple with VoIP policy questions, including which public-interest obligations should be required of VoIP providers and whether VoIP providers must comply with law enforcement wiretap requests.

Luckily, however, Congress and the FCC have charted a path for VoIP that has clarified much of the regulatory ambiguity without saddling the new technology with the legacy regulatory burden intended for monopoly telephone service. As a result, VoIP has flourished as a technology, has introduced competition to a previously stagnant market, and has lowered costs and improved access for consumers. Policymakers should seek to achieve the same with Bitcoin.

Bitcoin has the properties of an electronic payments system, a currency, and a commodity, among other things. As a result, it has already received scrutiny from several regulators. Below is an outline of some of the questions confronting these agencies as they prepare to regulate Bitcoin.

IS PRIVATE CURRENCY LEGAL?

One of the most common initial questions about Bitcoin is whether the online currency is legal, given the federal government's monopoly on issuing legal tender. The answer seems to be yes. The Constitution only prohibits the states from coining money.[169] Privately issued currencies are not forbidden, and in fact many local currencies are in circulation.[170] To promote local economies, businesspeople and lawmakers have developed several alternative currencies in recent years, such as the Cascadia Hour Exchange in Portland and Life Dollars in Bellingham, Washington.[171]

What private parties may not do is issue currency that resembles US money.[172] One notorious case is that of Bernard von NotHaus, who was convicted in 2011 after printing and distributing a gold-backed currency called the Liberty Dollar. His crime was not that he issued an alternative currency, but that it was similar in appearance to the US dollar and that von NotHaus attempted to spend his currency into circulation as dollars and encouraged others to do so as well.[173] In contrast, Bitcoin is in no danger of being confused with US currency.

FEDERAL MONEY LAUNDERING REGULATION

A business that transmits funds from one person to another is a money transmitter and, in 48 states and the District of Columbia, that person must obtain a license to operate.[174] Money transmitters are also subject to the Bank Secrecy Act (BSA) as implemented by regulations from FinCEN.[175] Additionally, the USA PATRIOT Act made it a criminal offense to operate an unlicensed money-transmission business.[176]

The purpose of state licensing of money transmission has traditionally been consumer protection.[177] Because money transmitters (such as money-order issuers) are typically not banks insured by the Federal Deposit Insurance Corporation (FDIC), consumers can be left holding the bag if a money transmitter does not forward the funds to the intended recipient. Licensing attempts to minimize this risk. Money-transmitter licensing in the United States became widespread after the widely publicized defaults of several money-order companies in the 1980s.[178]

The BSA, on the other hand, is intended to prevent or detect money laundering and terrorist financing.[179] It requires money transmitters and other financial institutions to register with FinCEN, implement anti–money-laundering programs, keep records of their customers, and report suspicious transactions and other data.

Bitcoin itself can't be said to be a money transmitter because it is a global peer-to-peer network rather than a company or legal entity. The question then is, do any of the actors in the Bitcoin ecosystem fit the statutory definitions of a money transmitter that would subject them to state and federal regulation?

In March 2013, FinCEN issued guidance on the application of the BSA to virtual currencies such as Bitcoin. The guidance defines three categories of persons potentially subject to its regulations as money transmitters:

> A *user* is a person that obtains virtual currency to purchase goods or services. An *exchanger* is a person engaged as a business in the exchange of virtual currency for real currency, funds, or other virtual currency. An *administrator* is a person engaged as a business in issuing (putting into circulation) a virtual currency, and who has the authority to redeem (to withdraw from circulation) such virtual currency.[180]

Those who meet the definition of an exchanger or administrator are considered by FinCEN to be money transmitters and must register with FinCEN and comply with the relevant record-keeping and reporting requirements—unless a person falls into one of the six exceptions outlined in previous FinCEN regulations.[181] Because states often look to FinCEN's determinations about which types of entities are or are not money transmitters, exchangers and administrators likely must obtain state money-transmitter licenses as well.

We can apply each of these definitions—and the various clarifications provided through FinCEN administrative rulings over time[182]—to persons in the Bitcoin ecosystem. The clearest definition is that of an *exchanger*. If one is in the business of exchanging dollars for bitcoins or vice versa, then we can conclude that one is a money transmitter under this guidance. Bitcoin exchanges that provide a platform for users to buy, sell, or convert bitcoins in other currencies would obviously fall into this category. But bitcoin processors, who merely accept and transmit funds between merchants and consumers necessary for the sale of goods and services, had understood their businesses to fall outside of the definition of exchangers because they qualify for some of the six exemptions under the definition of money transmitter.[183]

An administrative ruling from October of 2014 clarified that the "method of funding the transactions is not relevant to the definition of money transmitter" and therefore of an exchanger; a virtual currency business that exchanges currencies into other forms is considered an exchanger whether a business acts as a broker (matching pairs of buyers and sellers) or as a dealer (transacting directly with buyers or sellers from its own reserve).[184] Therefore, to their surprise, bitcoin payment processors that solely facilitated transfers between merchants and customers for the sale of goods and services might be subject to FinCEN regulation.[185] Only those bitcoin payment processors who facilitate transactions among parties that are all regulated under the BSA would be exempt from FinCEN oversight as an exchanger going forward.

Less straightforward is exactly who or what is considered a mere "user" of Bitcoin. The guidance states that if one obtains bitcoins "to purchase real or virtual goods or services," then one is not a money transmitter and not subject to FinCEN's regulations. An administrative ruling from January of 2014 clarified that a user is a person who "obtains virtual currency to purchase goods or services *on the user's own behalf*"[186] (emphasis added). But the new definition still does not explain how the law applies when one obtains bitcoins but *not* to purchase goods or services on one's own behalf.

Some other reasons why one might obtain bitcoins include (1) speculation that the price of bitcoins will go up, (2) simply because one trusts a virtual currency's stability more than that of a particular "real currency" (think of Argentina or Zimbabwe), or (3) because one wants to make a remittance to a family member overseas. All of these examples involve individuals using bitcoins on the "user's own behalf," but there has technically been no literal purchase of goods or services. Therefore, in none of these cases would Bitcoin users be assured that they are exempt from FinCEN's registration, record-keeping, and reporting requirements. This creates an uncertain regulatory environment that might unduly dampen use of Bitcoin.

Finally, the guidance notes that FinCEN regulations define currency as the currency of a state, and so the guidance also refers to this definition as "real currency."[187] It then develops a new concept that it calls "virtual currency" on which all the guidance is predicated.[188] The guidance defines virtual currency as "a medium of exchange that operates like a currency in some environments, but does not have all the attributes of real currency."[189] It goes on to introduce another concept by stating that there are different kinds of virtual currency and that the present guidance only extends to "convertible virtual currency," which it defines as one that "either has an equivalent value in real currency, or acts as a substitute for real currency."[190] While the definition of currency (aka real currency) was adopted through rulemaking, the other new and substantive concepts of virtual currency and convertible virtual currency exist only in the guidance. As a result, the guidance may be seen as encompassing new law and not merely interpretations of existing law or regulations, thus necessitating a rulemaking under the Administrative Procedure Act.

STATE MONEY-TRANSMISSION REGULATION

In addition to registering with FinCEN, money transmitters must also obtain a license from each of the 48 states that require it[191] and the District of Columbia before they are allowed to operate within those jurisdictions. Many of the states' licensing and reporting requirements are—on paper—quite similar to those outlined by other states. But this process becomes very expensive for new market entrants because money transmitters must repeat the process of applying and receiving certification from each of these governments in addition to submitting application fees to each state. The application and annual license fees for the states of Arizona, Connecticut, and Hawaii alone can reach respective maximums of $7,000, $5,650, and $30,000.[192] Many states require that money transmitters maintain a minimum net worth for businesses' principal offices and branch locations along with mandated security holdings. What's more, the requirements for each state can vary considerably and change often.[193] The overlapping fees and micromanaged business practices quickly add to the cost of business. Traditional money transmitters report spending up to five years to procure all of the necessary licenses from each of the states that require them.[194] Without smart policies, the virtual currency sphere risks a similar future.

The inefficient barriers to entry created by overlapping state money-transmission licensing requirements stand in stark contrast to the "permissionless innovation" ethos of the Bitcoin space.[195] Much of the beauty of Bitcoin lies in its openness to newcomers to build new services and improve upon old consumer needs. Entrepreneurs and technologists are free to tinker toward solutions that customers can choose to use or to ignore. Ideas and services stand on their own merits in the marketplace, not on businesses' ability to pay arbitrary filing fees or on their bureaucratic literacy. If thoughtlessly applied, state money-transmitter regulations could have the adverse impact of quashing the promising developments made possible with Bitcoin technology.[196]

Most states have not yet issued clarifications on how their money-transmitter licensing requirement will affect bitcoin businesses operating within their boundaries despite the emergence of a professional bitcoin industry. This has generated considerable legal uncertainty for bitcoin businesses that intend to comply with the laws but can glean little guidance from outdated statutory and regulatory language. So far, attorneys advising bitcoin businesses have attempted to overcome the prevailing legal murkiness by assessing the likely legal applicability and risk level before beginning operations in each state.[197] But this strategy is not foolproof: The Virginia-based and FinCEN-registered FastCash4Bitcoins shuttered operations in 2013 after receiving notice from the Commonwealth of Virginia that it ran afoul of state money-transmitter rules.[198] Bitcoin ventures with more resources have been better able to navigate the considerable regulatory requirements. Two of the best capitalized Bitcoin businesses, Coinbase and Circle, report that it cost each company roughly $2 million in fees and compliance exercises and several years to attain license from only 25 US states.[199]

A few states have started to refine how their money-transmission regulations will apply specifically to virtual currency companies. On one end of the spectrum, the New York Department of Financial Services (NYDFS) undertook a methodical and deeply involved process to develop new money-transmitter regulations to specifically address virtual currency businesses, soliciting months of public feedback with each new draft of the "BitLicense" that it released. On the other end is the state of Texas, which merely publicly confirmed that existing money-transmitter regulations indeed apply to virtual currency businesses in the same way as traditional money-transmission businesses.[200] The state of California, which is considering a legislative proposal to license digital currency businesses, sits somewhere between those extremes.

New York was one of the first states to develop a framework for regulating digital currencies. NYDFS Superintendent Benjamin Lawsky proactively forged an unprecedented approach to regulating virtual currency businesses starting in August of 2013 by issuing subpoenas to 22 bitcoin-related companies and venture capital firms,[201] holding public hearings,[202] developing regulatory proposals,[203] and even hosting "Ask Me Anything" (AMA) Q&A sessions on the popular content aggregator Reddit.[204] The first draft of the BitLicense proposal was released to the public on July 17, 2014.[205]

The initial proposal formally defined "Virtual Currency Business Activities" and laid out the licensing and oversight requirements that would be imposed on such businesses. But the early BitLicense language was so broad that it could have included such non–money transmitters as bitcoin miners, software developers, and wallet service providers.[206] Additionally, some initial BitLicense provisions would have all but made bitcoin transactions useless; for example, virtual currency businesses would have been required to collect the "physical addresses of the parties to the transaction" even when a party was not a direct customer of the service, thereby undermining the ease and affordability provided by Bitcoin. These and other textual issues were brought to NYDFS's attention by the over 3,700 public comments filed by industry, users, and academics regarding the draft BitLicense.[207]

NYDFS integrated some of this feedback into the final BitLicense regulation that was released on June 3, 2015.[208] It explicitly exempted software development, gift cards, gaming currencies, rewards credits, investment firms, and nonfinancial virtual currency transfers from BitLicense requirements, along with specifying a $5,000 application fee and a "conditional license" process for new startups. But problems remain.

Some of the revised language is still unclear. The definition for one type of Virtual Currency Business Activity requiring a BitLicense, "storing, holding, or maintaining custody or control of Virtual Currency on behalf of others," is *technically* incorrectly to applied to cryptocurrencies and worryingly vague.[209] Cryptocurrencies qua currencies are not "stored" or "held"—the private keys that control transactions are. Furthermore, it is not clear how the "maintaining custody or control" clause affects multisignature transactions wherein a bitcoin service might only control one of multiple private keys on behalf of a customer. Clarifying this language to specify Virtual Currency Business Activities in which businesses maintain the unilateral ability to execute or prevent transactions will prevent future confusion in application. Additionally, another type of Virtual Currency Business Activity, "controlling, administering, or issuing a Virtual Currency," could be amended to specify centralized virtual currencies and thereby clearly exempt virtual currency miners.

Other problems with the BitLicense could dampen innovation and competition. For example, the new "conditional license" language seeks to provide an on-ramp for new bitcoin businesses by authorizing the NYDFS to issue BitLicenses—at the superintendent's sole discretion—to companies that are not currently fully compliant. Providing an on-ramp is a worthy goal, but a discretionary process may have the adverse effect of introducing anticompetitive favoritism in licensing. An alternative on-ramp could exempt startups that process less than a certain amount in total transactions per year, or another such objective measure. Another problem is the BitLicense requirement that licensed businesses seek and receive official approval for any "new product, service, or activity, or to make a material change to an existing product, service, or activity." This kind of barrier would quickly overwhelm regulators and stymie normal business practices. More broadly, the BitLicense anti–money-laundering requirements would be the most onerous of its kind on the state level; they would duplicate and even exceed FinCEN requirements. Indeed, over a dozen Bitcoin businesses fled the state of New York once the final BitLicense regulations took effect.[210] Firms cited high compliance costs that exceeded several hundred thousand dollars[211] and the unjustifiable cybersecurity risks imposed by excessive customer-reporting requirements as the biggest flaws of the BitLicense.[212]

Amending these requirements to allow firms that are compliant with FinCEN AML to automatically secure BitLicense AML compliance—as all other states do—would streamline the regulations while ensuring the intended oversight. Finally, state money-transmitter rules that follow the BitLicense model should explicitly state that businesses that acquire a virtual currency license need not also acquire a traditional money-transmission license.

California provides a more promising case study for state money-transmission licensing of virtual currency firms. California's draft legislation to license digital currency businesses has been revised several times since it was first proposed by Assemblymember Matt Dababneh in February of 2015.[213] The current version is a significant improvement over the original draft, which did not specify which kinds of digital currency businesses would need to receive a license. The current draft legislation contains many strengths, and it does not duplicate onerous AML regulations like the revised BitLicense does. Rather, the California plan recognizes that FinCEN-registered virtual currency businesses are already compliant with federal AML law. The legislation also outlines a precise and appropriate definition of a "virtual currency business," which includes firms that "maintain full custody or control of virtual currency on behalf of others." The precise "full custody or control" language clearly and appropriately exempts partial custody arrangements—such as multisignature transactions—from the regulations. Additionally, the legislation specifically exempts other virtual currency players who share no role in unilaterally storing customer funds, such as software developers and payee agents. By tailoring regulations specifically to only the appropriate types of firm, the California legislation achieves an impressive balance between protecting consumers and fostering an environment for innovation.

Other states will surely look to the examples of New York and California as they begin to adopt their own money-transmitter rules to bitcoin businesses. Obviously, the California model will be far more attractive to innovation-minded policymakers. However, those living in states with appropriate virtual currency regulations may still suffer from diminished opportunities if enough other states promulgate ill-considered or onerous regulations. Small startups may simply be unable to stay in US markets if the additive compliance costs across states are too high.

Some believe that US states can maximize both the opportunities and consumer safety of virtual currency business ventures by harmoniously standardizing virtual currency money-transmission regulations across jurisdictions. The US Conference of State Bank Supervisors (CSBS) is one group that has worked to develop a framework for state regulators to consult when considering how to approach virtual currency businesses. In theory, consistent and appropriate regulations across the states could indeed limit the costs to new bitcoin businesses. The CSBS's policy goal—that "activities involving fiat currencies that are otherwise subject to state laws should be covered if undertaken using virtual currency"—is a reasonable approach that could improve virtual currency competitiveness and service in the United States. Unfortunately, the language of the final CSBS framework, which was released in September of 2015, would undermine this goal in practice. The "covered activities" that would be regulated under the CSBS framework include any "services that facilitate the third party exchange, storage, and/or transmission of virtual currency."[214] This unnecessarily broad language could be interpreted to cover the activities of a wide range of service providers who would not be regulated if involved in the same activities using fiat currencies, for example, Internet Service Providers, software developers, or web hosting services.[215] The various state regulators who choose to follow the CSBS guidelines may therefore implement regulations that are wildly different and ultimately burdensome to virtual currency businesses and customers. The shortcomings of the final CSBS framework highlight the difficulties of precisely and appropriately coordinating state money-transmission regulations, even when undertaken by a qualified organization with admirable goals.

Ideally, states could develop reciprocity or sharing agreements to overcome the regulatory duplication problem. For example, some have suggested encouraging license-sharing arrangements for money transmitters,[216] where an established licensee partners with a new bitcoin business to allow quick and compliant operation. Virtual currency firms would benefit from a clear and accessible on-ramp to innovate and experiment while regulators and consumers would have peace of mind knowing that these new businesses are guided by the seasoned professional compliance team of their established licensee partner. Others propose a uniform license that could authorize operations in many or all states that require it.[217] Similarly, individual states could decide to form reciprocity arrangements with one another or with groups of other states. For example, a state could decide to allow any virtual currency firm that attains a license from, say, California, to legally operate within its own jurisdiction. This kind of arrangement could cut down on the regulatory overhead while ensuring both consumer protection and innovation. However, for reciprocity and sharing agreements to be effective, they will require a level of interstate consensus that may be difficult to achieve without federal preemption. State money-transmitter licensing laws remain one of the largest legal uncertainties facing bitcoin businesses in the United States and will continue to generate debate as more states weigh in.

TAX TREATMENT

Because of its versatility, there are many ways that the Internal Revenue Service could have proceeded to classify bitcoins for tax purposes. Before the IRS clarified that virtual currencies will be taxed as property,[218] there was much discussion about the implications of the eventual decision.[219] Whichever category the IRS determined would be best applied to Bitcoin would have pronounced effects on industry practices and consumer use. The two most likely candidates for bitcoin taxation were "currency" and "property."

If the IRS had categorized bitcoin as currency, gains from trading bitcoins for dollars would have been taxed just as the gains from trading British pounds and Japanese yen, which are taxed as ordinary income at marginal rates. Currency transactions, however, enjoy a de minimis personal use exemption for transactions under $1,000. In the end, the IRS chose to classify bitcoin as property,[220] which is taxed at capital gains rates that are typically lower than marginal tax rates. On the other hand, however, there is no de minimis personal use exemption for property. In fact, the decision was largely out of the IRS's hands: By statute, the "currency" is limited to the "coin and currency of the United States, or of any other country."[221] Because bitcoin is not issued by any country, it cannot be considered currency.

One consequence of this decision is that bitcoin users owe tax on any gains they realize *any time* they dispose of bitcoins. For example, Alice would owe taxes when she sells bitcoins to Bob for $10,000 that she had bought for $7,000, or when she uses bitcoins to buy a cup of coffee if the market value of those bitcoins has risen since she purchased them. Technically, bitcoin users must meticulously keep track of all gains and losses—even on small daily transactions—for tax reporting. Consumer service providers, like Coinbase, have attempted to ease the cost of tax reporting by providing tax payment reports for customers.[222] Individuals who hold their own bitcoins, though, would need to have the foresight and skill to manage these requirements on their own.

But this tax arrangement could also end up imposing significant costs on an unexpected group: the IRS itself. Because the IRS lacks a surefire way to track and audit individual bitcoin users and transactions, the final compliance of many taxable transactions will ultimately rely on the knowledge and cooperation of the users themselves. The high compliance costs imposed on users and the weak investigatory tools available to the IRS will likely be areas that are addressed by future IRS guidance.

COMMODITY FUTURES REGULATION

By their nature, bitcoins can be conceived of as a commodity or as a currency—or as a bit of both. Indeed, economist George Selgin has called Bitcoin "synthetic-commodity money."[223] This has attracted the attention of the Commodity Futures Trading Commission, which has the authority to regulate commodity futures and the markets in which they trade, as well as to regulate some foreign-exchange instruments.[224]

Echoing other agencies' determinations that virtual currencies do not most closely fit the definition of foreign currencies, the CFTC is proceeding to regulate bitcoin derivatives under its commodity futures trading oversight authority. The Commodity Exchange Act (CEA), passed in 1936, defines commodities as all "goods and articles . . . and all services, rights, and interests . . . in which contracts for future delivery are presently or in the future dealt in," except onions and "motion picture box office receipts."[225] Therefore, bitcoins can clearly qualify as a commodity because they are articles that can be traded and made subject to futures contracts.

The CFTC's authority is not over commodities themselves, however, but commodity *futures*, which are tradable contracts to purchase or sell commodities at a certain date for a certain price. As CFTC Chairman Timothy Massad stated in Senate testimony, CFTC regulation of bitcoins "will depend on the facts and circumstances pertaining to any particular activity in question."[226] CFTC authority over commodity futures includes such a broad expanse of underlying assets as "Treasury securities, interest rate indices, stock market indices, currencies, electricity, and heating degree days" in addition to virtual currencies.[227] An exchange of bitcoins for dollars or other national currency, however, typically occurs instantaneously, and not as part of a futures contract. Therefore, CFTC regulation of bitcoins in all uses *as commodities* is limited.

The CFTC has been proactive in developing a flexible regulatory framework appropriate for commodity futures trading involving virtual currencies. CFTC Commissioner Mark Wetjen penned an op-ed in the *Wall Street Journal* emphasizing Bitcoin's "potential to act as a disruptive innovation" and recognizing the need for a robust derivatives market to help "hedge exposures to fluctuations in its value."[228] Wetjen called upon regulatory bodies to follow the CFTC's approach in creating an adaptable and adequate regulatory framework that would build consumer confidence without inhibiting innovation and development. More recently, CFTC Commissioner J. Christopher Giancarlo echoed Wetjen's message by praising the innovative benefits of blockchain applications and reminding regulators to embrace a "do not harm" approach to blockchain technologies.[229]

After months of meetings with TeraExchange representatives, the CFTC granted a temporary registration to the bitcoin swap execution facility in September of 2013, citing its authority to regulate commodity futures under the Commodity Exchange Act.[230] A year later, TeraExchange, which lists a bilateral, nondeliverable, noncleared swap contract that is based on a proprietary index of bitcoin prices that is settled in US dollars,[231] received full CFTC approval to officially launch the first licensed bitcoin derivate trading platform.[232]Additionally, the CFTC has begun to bring enforcement actions against virtual currency futures and swaps trading platforms that operate without registration. The regulatory body settled its first case against an unregistered derivatives trading platform called Derivabit in September of 2015.[233] The platform was ordered to cease and desist after it was found to be illegally offering Bitcoin options and trading swaps without first registering with the CFTC. The CFTC's order reiterated its position that Bitcoin and other virtual currencies are indeed a commodity covered by the CEA and therefore subject to CFTC oversight and registration requirements.

The CFTC has also claimed a broader power to oversee Bitcoin and virtual currencies to prevent such "price manipulation" more generally. Commissioner Wetjen has stated that CFTC authority is not limited to regulating against market manipulation by licensed platforms like TeraExchange; it also includes the authority to "bring enforcement against any type of manipulation."[234] The 2010 Dodd-Frank Act extended new authority to the CFTC to prohibit price manipulation, which occurs when any person, directly or indirectly, intentionally manipulates or attempts to manipulate the price of any swap, commodity, or futures contract.[235] This authority has only been used once so far, in April of 2015, when the CFTC launched a lawsuit against Kraft Foods Group and Mondelez Global LLC over alleged price manipulation of wheat prices by purchasing substantial futures contracts in 2011.[236] Commissioner Wetjen's comments raise the possibility that this channel could expand the CFTC's authority over Bitcoin beyond merely overseeing futures contracts based on bitcoins to include any such bitcoin transactions that the CFTC determines to be engaging in price manipulation.[237] However, given that the CFTC has so far only meagerly applied this authority, such expansive application to bitcoin transactions is unlikely.

SECURITIES REGULATION

As mentioned earlier, the early Bitcoin ecosystem harbored a number of unregistered securities exchanges in which traders could buy and sell shares of companies or mutual funds for bitcoins.[238] The first and most popular of these new ventures, the Global Bitcoin Stock Exchange, hosted 10 stock offerings valued at a cumulative sum of over $650,000 at its peak of activity in May of 2012. But the freedom that generated these successful experiments also created the potential for fraudulent activity, as the infamous case of the Bitcoin Savings and Trust illustrates. Additionally, virtual currency securities markets knowingly operated in an incredibly tenuous legal area from the start. Because these platforms were centralized services that merely used Bitcoin to fund transactions, market operators were legally on the line in the eyes of law, even if not in their own minds. Another market, BTC-TC, acknowledged its dubious legality in its FAQ for customers, instructing users that nothing traded on the market should be considered real, that the use of this site was for "educational and entertainment purposes only," and that customers have "ZERO RECOURSE" if an asset issuer defaults or absconds with investor funds.[239] Even exchange operators recognized that it was only a matter of time before such securities platforms came under SEC regulation; indeed, the operator of GLBSE abruptly shuttered market trading after his lawyers convinced him the platform ran grossly afoul of securities regulations.

The SEC exerted authority over bitcoin securities markets when knowledge of cryptocurrencies became mainstream in 2013, citing its responsibilities in proposing and enforcing federal securities rules and regulating securities exchanges. The agency's first comment about virtual currencies came in the form of an investor alert from the SEC Office of Investor Education and Advocacy in June of 2013; it warns consumers about cryptocurrency-based Ponzi schemes.[240] Citing Bitcoin's enhanced privacy features and limited oversight, the document urges investors to be vigilant against fraudulent investment vehicles promising high returns on unregistered trading platforms. It unequivocally states,

> Any investment in securities in the United States remains subject to the jurisdiction of the SEC regardless of whether the investment is made in U.S. dollars or a virtual currency. In particular, individuals selling investments are typically subject to federal or state licensing requirements.[241]

This warning proved prescient. On July 23, 2013, the SEC filed a complaint against the owner of BTCST,

Trendon Shavers, for running an illegal Ponzi scheme.[242] The scheme collected bitcoins from investors, which Shavers would then "sell to a local group of people" and profit from the arbitrage, promising yields of up to 1 percent per day. One of the most popular listings on GLBSE, BTCST attracted investments of up to $7 million at its peak.[243] The SEC had a different interpretation of the setup. "In reality," the SEC's complaint alleged, "the BTCST offering was a sham and a Ponzi scheme whereby Shavers used new BTCST investors' BTC to pay the promised returns on outstanding BTCST investments and misappropriated BTCST investors' BTC for his personal use."[244]

Shavers' defense disputed that his activities fell under SEC jurisdiction. Pointing to court precedent that the Securities Act only authorizes the regulation of instruments that involve the investment of money in a common enterprise with the expectation of profits derived solely from the efforts of others, Shavers argued that Bitcoin is not money and therefore bitcoin-denominated instruments do not fall under SEC regulation. The court disagreed, finding that bitcoins are indeed money. Therefore, the BTCST investment met the definition of investment contracts subject to SEC regulation and Shavers was found guilty of the charges. The BTCST episode indicates that securities trading is unlikely to escape SEC regulation by denominating securities in virtual currency.[245]

The SEC is also pursuing retroactive enforcement of securities regulations. The BTC-TC marketplace was found in violation of SEC regulations on December 8, 2014,[246] more than a year after the platform was closed due to the operators' concerns about legal compliance.[247] The SEC charged that programmer and operator Ethan Burnside operated securities trading platforms without appropriately registering them as broker-dealers or stock markets with the SEC. Emphasizing the necessity of SEC registration, SEC representative Andrew Calamari reiterated that "no exemption applies simply because an entity is operating on the Internet or using a virtual currency in securities transactions." Other unregistered bitcoin securities platforms, and perhaps even the decentralized application platforms like Ethereum that we will soon discuss, may face such retroactive scrutiny from the SEC as well.

Bitcoin securities ventures now seek regulatory approval before beginning trading. The proposed Winklevoss Bitcoin Trust ETF began the long process of registering with the SEC in July of 2013,[248] with the intention of listing 1 million shares for sale when approved. In contrast, the Bitcoin Investment Trust (BIT) fund decided to pursue the less onerous process of regulation under the Financial Industry Regulatory Authority (FINRA), the largest independent securities regulator in the United States.[249] Because FINRA is regulated by the SEC, BIT would not need to secure additional SEC regulation if properly registered and overseen by FINRA. However, companies that seek to substitute FINRA regulation for the more involved SEC registration process must structure their firms in a way that SEC-regulated firms need not. BIT, for example, secured FINRA oversight through a loophole that allows fund holders to sell their shares after one year. Firms' decisions over which regulatory route to pursue may depend on the unique cost-benefit analysis for each approach.

A growing number of projects have adopted the decentralized application platform (DAP) model of development.[250] This new method of project funding may also have regulatory implications. Projects that have employed the DAP model, such as Ethereum and Maidsafe, boast the ambitious goal of building a single platform that can provide not only distributed transactions like Bitcoin but also a self-contained ecosystem that will allow users to dynamically develop software and products that will eventually replace the Internet itself. In these initiatives, the creation of a new blockchain currency serves a dual purpose. Blockchains are employed to run the actual software while a new cryptocurrency token is issued to the public to crowdfund investment capital. DAP currency launches serve as a kind of initial public offering (IPO) for network investment: Money raised from the sale of native DAP cryptocurrency tokens is used to fund development and testing of the underlying protocol. DAP currency launches have tended to suffer from "technical difficulties" more often than not: MaidSafe's Mastercoin immediately suffered a liquidity crash upon launch,[251] and Ethereum's ether sale was postponed for months because the software had not been fully developed as planned.[252]

The SEC may decide to more actively explore whether they have jurisdiction over such arrangements. In doing so, it will employ the "Howey Test" for determining whether such tokens can be investment contract.[253] Applying this test, the SEC should find that larger and more decentralized cryptocurrencies like Bitcoin, as well as the pegged cryptocurrencies of sidechains and distributed computing platforms like Ethereum, do not easily fit the definition of a regulated security.[254] The SEC, however, should be able to find that more-centrally organized and questionably marketed "scamcoins" can be categorized as securities.[255]

FEDERAL CONSUMER PROTECTION REGULATION

The final possible vector for regulation of Bitcoin under existing law that we will consider is regulation and oversight by the Consumer Financial Protection Bureau. The CFPB issued a consumer advisory about Bitcoin and virtual currencies in August of 2014, warning potential users about the risks of volatility, hacking, scamming, and lost or deleted private keys.[256] Consumers who experience these problems with virtual currency products or third-party service providers can now submit complaints to the CFPB for investigation; such complaints will also be added to the agency's broader database of consumer complaints.

Additionally, the CFPB may pursue Bitcoin regulation under the Electronic Fund Transfer Act (EFTA)[257] and its application through the Federal Reserve's Regulation E.[258] The purpose of the EFTA is to establish the respective rights and responsibilities of consumers and financial institutions in electronic fund transfers.[259] Like the other laws and regulations we have seen, the EFTA does not seem to anticipate a decentralized virtual currency like Bitcoin. However, a December 2014 CFPB notice of proposed rulemaking relating to prepaid cards indicates that digital currencies like Bitcoin may nonetheless be subject to EFTA regulation.[260]

The EFTA defines electronic fund transfers as "any transfer of funds, other than a transaction originated by check, draft, or similar paper instrument, which is initiated through an electronic terminal, telephonic instrument, or computer or magnetic tape so as to order, instruct, or authorize a financial institution to debit or credit an account."[261] It further defines "financial institution" as "a State or National bank, a State or Federal savings and loan association, a mutual savings bank, a State or Federal credit union, or any other person who, directly or indirectly, holds an account belonging to a consumer."[262] These definitions, and the regulations they undergird, assume that electronic fund transfers will necessarily involve "financial institutions" and "accounts." Bitcoin, however, runs counter to that notion.

The Bitcoin system itself does not qualify as a financial institution because, as noted earlier, it is not a company or legal entity but instead a global peer-to-peer network. As a result, a Bitcoin address with which bitcoins are associated on the network cannot be said to be an account of a financial institution. Furthermore, as noted above in the technical discussion of how bitcoins are transferred between addresses, in the Bitcoin system there are no financial institutions or other third parties of any kind that "debit or credit an account." Electronic fund transfers between addresses are carried out by users alone, who sign a transaction with the private key associated with a Bitcoin address under their control. The Bitcoin network merely confirms that the transaction is legitimate.

While many users keep the wallet files containing their private keys on their own computers or other devices,[263] some delegate securing their keys to online wallet services.[264] Such third-party wallet services, like Blockchain or Mycelium, often also provide greater ease of use than desktop Bitcoin software. Users typically create an "account" on such a wallet service, and their Bitcoin addresses are associated with those accounts. It is conceivable that such online services could fit the definition of "financial institution" under the EFTA, and thus be subject to the regulation.

Finally, new rules from the Consumer Financial Protection Bureau amending Regulation E target remittance-transfer providers, and they may apply to bitcoin-based services.

The regulations require remittance providers to disclose exchange rates and fees associated with international transfers, and to investigate and remediate processing errors.[265] They also require that consumers be afforded 30 minutes or more to cancel a transfer.[266] This requirement can be seen as incompatible with the Bitcoin protocol because standard bitcoin transactions are irreversible.[267] One way for intermediaries to comply with this regulation might be to delay the execution of transactions.

VI. POLICY RECOMMENDATIONS

As we have seen, Bitcoin does not easily fit into existing regulatory boxes. That is often the hallmark of a disruptive technology. Indeed Bitcoin is a revolutionary technical achievement that heralds amazing potential benefits to human welfare. However, like any technology that can be used for good, it can also be used for ill. The challenge for policymakers will be to foster Bitcoin's beneficial uses while minimizing its negative consequences. We have some recommendations to help policymakers meet this challenge.

DON'T RESTRICT BITCOIN

Because Bitcoin is essentially online cash, some who trade in drugs and other illicit goods online have found it to be an ideal medium of exchange.[268] Confronted with this fact, the initial impulse of some policymakers will be to call for restrictions on the technology.[269] There are many good reasons, however, to resist such an impulse.

First, as a technology, Bitcoin is neither good nor bad; it is neutral. Paper dollar bills, like bitcoins, can be used in illicit transactions, yet we do not consider outlawing paper bills. We only prohibit their *illicit use*. Furthermore, there is only anecdotal evidence about the extent to which bitcoins are utilized in criminal transactions. It would be wise to put the criminal use of the technology in perspective alongside its legitimate uses. As the bitcoin economy grows, legitimate uses of bitcoins will likely dwarf criminal transactions,[270] just as we see with paper dollar bills.

Second, any attempt to restrict Bitcoin technology will only harm legitimate uses while leaving illicit uses largely unaffected. Because it is a decentralized global network, Bitcoin is virtually impossible to shut down. There is no Bitcoin company or other entity that can be targeted. Instead, Bitcoin and its ledger exist only in the distributed peer-to-peer network created by its users. As with BitTorrent, the peer-to-peer file-sharing service, taking down any of the individual computers that make up the peer-to-peer system would have little effect on the rest of the network. Therefore, making the use of Bitcoin illegal would not undermine the network; it would only serve to ensure that law-abiding users are denied access to the technology. As a result, society would forgo the many potential benefits of Bitcoin without seeing any drop in criminal use.

Third, if Bitcoin were prohibited, the government would forego the opportunity to regulate intermediaries in the bitcoin economy, such as exchangers and money transmitters. The government's interests in detecting and preventing money laundering and terrorist financing would be better advanced, not by prohibiting the technology, but by requiring intermediaries to keep records and report suspicious activities, just as traditional financial institutions do. Again, restricting the use of Bitcoin will only ensure that criminals alone will use the technology.

Any illicit intermediaries that emerge, such as exchanges and payment processors, will be unregulated.

Finally, even if the United States prohibited the use of Bitcoin, it is likely that many other countries would not, recognizing the technology's many potential benefits. The Finnish central bank, for example, has stated that the digital currency is not illegal,[271] and as a result many Finnish businesses have begun to accept bitcoins.[272] By prohibiting Bitcoin use, the United States could put itself at an international competitive disadvantage in the development and use of what may be the next-generation payments system.

CLARIFY REGULATION AND ENCOURAGE FURTHER DEVELOPMENT

Rather than overreact to illicit uses of Bitcoin, policymakers would be wise to take a calm and careful approach to the challenges posed by the new technology. Doing so would allow law enforcement to pursue its interests in detecting and preventing money laundering and terrorist financing while ensuring that society does not forgo Bitcoin's many benefits. Luckily, regulators to date have taken such a cautious approach by slowly integrating Bitcoin into the existing financial regulatory framework. Policymakers can take a few basic steps to maintain the right balance.

In the short term, state governments should decide how they will approach money-transmission licensing of bitcoin businesses. Whether they decide to craft new regulations specifically addressing virtual currency transmitters, as New York has done, or simply adapt existing money-transmission rules to apply to the unique attributes of virtual currencies, as Texas has, states should clarify their policies as soon as possible so that regulatory uncertainty does not thwart the innovative capacities of this developing industry.[273] Furthermore, states should take care that licensing requirements are no more onerous on virtual currency businesses than they are on traditional money transmitters. Instituting nondiscretionary and less burdensome on-ramp tracks for new businesses will encourage startup formation while maintaining adequate oversight. A licensing ecosystem that maintains interstate consistency while minimizing the additive costs on businesses, as outlined in the preliminary draft of the proposed CSBS framework for state money-transmission licensing,[274] will provide states and their constituents with the dual benefits of consumer protection and competitive financial services markets.

In the long term, policymakers should better define Bitcoin's broader regulatory status. As we have seen, the digital currency does not comfortably fit any existing classification or legal definition. It is neither a foreign currency nor a traditional commodity; nor is it simply a payments network. Consequently, applying existing rules to Bitcoin could unduly impede Bitcoin's legitimate development without any attendant gains to law enforcement or consumer welfare. As a result, policymakers may want to consider developing a new category that takes into account the technology's unique nature. For example, the IRS may consider how to provide more clarity on the tax treatment of bitcoin transactions, perhaps by establishing a new tax category for virtual currencies that combines the de minimis exemption of low transaction amounts through currency taxation with the low capital gains tax rates of property taxation. In general, regulators should also carefully consider and distinguish what regulation, if any, bitcoin exchanges, payment processors, and users should face.

Finally, policymakers should not only allow Bitcoin's development to continue unimpeded, they should help foster its growth by revisiting existing regulatory barriers. One of the greatest obstacles to Bitcoin's legitimate adoption is the requirement that businesses engaging in money transmission acquire a license from each state. This is a duplicative, laborious, and expensive process that presents a barrier to interstate commerce without much benefit to consumers. Federal lawmakers and regulators should consider whether preemption is necessary.

VII. CONCLUSION

Bitcoin is an exciting innovation that has the potential to greatly improve human welfare and jump-start beneficial and potentially revolutionary developments in payments, communications, and business. Bitcoin's clever use of public-key encryption and peer-to-peer networking solves the double-spending problem that had previously made decentralized digital currencies impossible. These properties combine to create a payment system that could lower transaction costs in business and remittances, alleviate poverty, provide an escape from capital controls and monetary mismanagement, allow for legitimate financial privacy online, and spur new financial innovations. On the other hand, as digital cash, Bitcoin can be used for money laundering and illicit trade. However, banning Bitcoin is not the solution to ending money laundering and illicit trade, just as banning cash is not a solution to these same ills.

Bitcoin could ultimately fail as an experimental digital currency and payment system. An unanticipated problem could arise and undermine the bitcoin economy. A superior cryptocurrency could outcompete and replace Bitcoin, or it could simply fizzle out as a fad. The possibilities for failure are endless, but one reason for failure should not be that policymakers did not understand its workings and its potential. We are ultimately advocating, not for Bitcoin, but for innovation. It is important that policymakers allow this experimentation to continue. Policymakers should work to clarify how Bitcoin is regulated and to normalize its regulation so that we have the opportunity to learn just how innovative Bitcoin can be.

NOTES

1. Financial information provided at bitcoincharts.com estimates total market capitalization to be $6,454,987,805 as of April 4, 2016.

2. Sarah E. Needleman and Spencer E. Ante, "Bitcoin Startups Begin to Attract Real Cash," *Wall Street Journal*, May 8, 2013, http://online.wsj.com/article/SB10001424127887336876045784690123752699952.html.

3. "Bitcoin Venture Investments," *CoinDesk*, accessed February 1, 2016, http://www.coindesk.com/bitcoin-venture-capital/.

4. Goldman Sachs notes that "Innovations in network technology and cryptography could change the speed and mechanics of moving money." See James Schneider and S.K. Prasad Borra, *The Future of Finance: Redefining "The Way We Pay" in the Next Decade* (report, Goldman Sachs, March 10, 2015).

5. A group of investors, including traditional banks and the New York Stock Exchange, recently invested $75 million in the bitcoin payment processor Coinbase. See Paul Vigna and Michael J. Casey, "Coinbase Raises $75 Million in Funding Round," *Wall Street Journal*, January 20, 2015, http://www.wsj.com/articles/coinbase-raises-75-million-in-funding-round-1421762403.

6. François R. Velde, "Bitcoin: A Primer" (Essays on Issues No. 317, Federal Reserve Bank of Chicago, December 2013), https://www.chicagofed.org/publications/chicago-fed-letter/2013/december-317.

7. US Department of the Treasury, Financial Crimes and Enforcement Network, "Application of FinCEN's Regulations to Persons Administering, Exchanging, or Using Virtual Currencies" (Guidance FIN-2013-G001, March 18, 2013), http://fincen.gov/statutes_regs/guidance/html/FIN-2013-G001.html.

8. Jennifer Shasky Calvery, Asset Forfeiture and Money Laundering Section, Criminal Division, Department of Justice, "Combating Transnational Organized Crime: International Money Laundering as a Threat to Our

Financial Systems" (Statement for the Record before the Subcommittee on Crime, Terrorism, and Homeland Security of the House Committee on the Judiciary, February 8, 2012), http://www.justice.gov/ola/testimony/112-2/02-08-12-crm-shasky-calvery-testimony.pdf.

9. Internal Revenue Service, "Virtual Currency Guidance," Notice 2014-21, April 14, 2014, https://www.irs.gov/irb/2014-16_IRB/ar12.html.

10. Timothy Massad, US Commodity Futures Trading Commission, Testimony before the Senate Committee on Agriculture, Nutrition, and Forestry, December 10, 2014, http://www.cftc.gov/PressRoom/SpeechesTestimony/opamassad-6.

11. Consumer Financial Protection Bureau, "Risks to Consumers Posed by Virtual Currencies," August 2014, http://www.consumerfinance.gov/blog/consumer-advisory-virtual-currencies-and-what-you-should-know-about-them/.

12. Securities and Exchange Commission, "Ponzi Schemes Using Virtual Currencies," May 2014, https://www.sec.gov/oiea/investor-alerts-bulletins/investoralertsia_bitcoin.html.

13. Federal Election Commission, "Political Committee May Accept Bitcoins as Contributions," *FEC Advisory Opinion, AO 2014-02*, May 8, 2014, http://www.fec.gov/pages/fecrecord/2014/june/ao2014-02.shtml.

14. Nathaniel Popper and Sydney Ember, "Winklevoss Twins Aim to Take Bitcoin Mainstream," *DealBook, New York Times*, January 22, 2015, http://dealbook.nytimes.com/2015/01/22/winklevoss-twins-aim-to-take-bitcoin-mainstream-with-a-regulated-exchange/.

15. US Commodity Futures Trading Commission, "CFTC Issues Notice of Temporary Registration as a Swap Execution Facility to TeraExchange, LLC," September 19, 2013, http://www.cftc.gov/PressRoom/PressReleases/pr6698-13.

16. 23 NY C.R.R. 200, http://www.dfs.ny.gov/legal/regulations/adoptions/dfsp200t.pdf.

17. Pete Rizzo, "California Bill Proposes License Requirement for Bitcoin Businesses," *CoinDesk*, March 3, 2015, http://www.coindesk.com/california-bill-license-require-bitcoin-business/.

18. David Chaum, "Achieving Electronic Privacy," *Scientific American*, August 1992, 96–101.

19. Christof Paar, Jan Pelzl, and Bart Preneel, "Introduction to Public-Key Cryptography," in *Understanding Cryptography: A Textbook for Students and Practitioners*, eds. Christof Paar and Jan Pelzl (New York: Springer-Verlag, 2010). Sample available at http://wiki.crypto.rub.de/Buch/download/Understanding-Cryptography-Chapter6.pdf.

20. "Address," *Bitcoin Wiki*, accessed January 28, 2016, https://en.bitcoin.it/wiki/Address.

21. "Wallet," *Bitcoin Wiki*, accessed January 28, 2016, https://en.bitcoin.it /wiki/Wallet.
22. Miners tend to be ordinary computer enthusiasts, but as mining becomes more difficult and expensive, the activity will likely become somewhat professionalized. For more information, see Alec Liu, "A Guide to Bitcoin Mining," *Motherboard*, March 22, 2013, http://motherboard.vice.com /blog/a-guide-to-bitcoin-mining-why-someone-bought-a-1500-bitcoin -miner-on-ebay-for-20600.
23. Ken Tindell, "Geeks Love the Bitcoin Phenomenon Like They Loved the Internet in 1995," *Business Insider*, April 5, 2013, http://www .businessinsider.com/how-bitcoins-are-mined-and-used-2013-4.
24. Nermin Hajdarbegovic, "Bitcoin Price Decline Sparks Rare Mining Difficulty Drop," *CoinDesk*, December 3, 2014, http://www.coindesk.com /bitcoin-price-decline-sparks-rare-mining-difficulty-drop/.
25. Note that this might be a boon to economic researchers.
26. "Address," *Bitcoin Wiki*.
27. Elli Androulaki et al., "Evaluating User Privacy in Bitcoin," *IACR Cryptology ePrint Archive* 596 (2012), http://fc13.ifca.ai/proc/1-3.pdf.
28. Fergal Reid and Martin Harrigan, "An Analysis of Anonymity in the Bitcoin System," in *Security and Privacy in Social Networks*, eds. Yaniv Altshuler et al. (New York: Springer, 2013), http://arxiv.org/pdf /1107.4524v2.pdf.
29. Dorit Ron and Adi Shamir, "Quantitative Analysis of the Full Bitcoin Transaction Graph," *IACR Cryptology ePrint Archive* 584 (2012), http:// eprint.iacr.org/2012/584.pdf.
30. Entity merging is the process of observing two or more public keys used as an input to one transaction at the same time. In this way, even if a user has several different public keys, an observer can gradually link them together and remove the ostensible anonymity that multiple public keys is thought to provide.
31. Micha Ober, Stefan Katzenbeisser, and Kay Hamacher, "Structure and Anonymity of the Bitcoin Transaction Graph," *Future Internet* 5, no. 2 (2013), http://www.mdpi.com/1999-5903/5/2/237.
32. Andy Greenberg, "Prosecutors Trace $13.4 M in Bitcoins from the Silk Road to Ulbricht's Laptop," *Wired*, January 29, 2015, http://www.wired .com/2015/01/prosecutors-trace-13-4-million-bitcoins-silk-road-ulbrichts -laptop/.
33. Jerry Brito, "Silk Road Corruption Case Shows How Law Enforcement Uses Bitcoin," *Coin Center*, April 1, 2015, https://coincenter.org/2015/04 /silk-road-corruption-case-shows-how-law-enforcement-uses-bitcoin/.
34. For example, one developer is exploring cryptographic tools to improve the privacy and security of Bitcoin. See Greg Maxwell, "Confidential

Transactions," June 2015, https://people.xiph.org/~greg/confidential_values.txt.

35. Mining rewards currently offset enough of miners' costs to render most Bitcoin transactions very cheap, if not free. Users can add a higher transaction fee if they wish to incentivize miners to prioritize their transaction. After the 21 million currency cap is reached, and miners no longer receive freshly minted bitcoins as a reward, all transactions will likely incur an extra transaction fee. However, Bitcoin fees could still be cheaper than or comparable to those of third-party payment processors even after the currency cap is reached, and they still would provide the added benefit of decentralized clearing. For more, see Kerem Kaskaloglu, "Near Zero Bitcoin Transaction Fees Cannot Last Forever" (working paper presented at the International Conference on Digital Security and Forensics, VSB Technical University of Ostrava, Czech Republic, June 2014), http://sdiwc.net/digital-library/near-zero-bitcoin-transaction-fees-cannot-last-forever.html.

36. Micropayments are tiny transactions that allow people to pay for metered services like pay-per-minute Wi-Fi or streaming services. Because Bitcoin transaction fees are currently much lower than those for traditional payment options like credit cards, many entrepreneurs have looked to Bitcoin as a cheap and easy metering service. For example, the Streamium and Faradam projects allow people to broadcast tutorials, entertainment, and news while charging viewers a certain small amount of bitcoins per unit of time. However, some worry that the blockchain would be put under heavy strain if enough micropayment transactions dominate the network. Accordingly, some developers are working on technical fixes to facilitate micropayments without burdening the network, e.g., the Bitcoinj micropayment channel. See Daniel Cawrey, "The Promise of Bitcoin Micropayments: Corporations, Incentives, and Altcoins," *CoinDesk*, February 11, 2014, http://www.coindesk.com/promise-bitcoin-micropayments-corporations-incentives-altcoins/; Pete Rizzo, "Bitcoin Micropayment Service Targets Global Freelancers," *CoinDesk*, August 25, 2015, http://www.coindesk.com/bitcoin-micropayments-faraday-freelance-market/; David Gilson, "Bitcoin Client Bitcoinj Implements Bitcoin Micropayments," *CoinDesk*, July 1, 2013, http://www.coindesk.com/bitcoin-client-bitcoinj-implements-bitcoin-micropayments/.

37. Pete Rizzo, "BitPay Raises $30 Million in Record-Breaking Bitcoin Funding Round," *CoinDesk*, May 13, 2014, http://www.coindesk.com/bitpay-closes-30-million-funding-round-led-by-index-ventures/.

38. Vigna and Casey, "Coinbase Raises $75 Million."

39. Michael Carney, "BitPagos allows Latin American merchants to avoid sky high payment fees by accepting bitcoin," *Pando*, June 17, 2014, https://pando.com/2014/06/17/bitpagos-allow-latinam-merchants-to-avoid-sky-high-payment-fees-by-accepting-bitcoin/.

40. Bailey Reutzel, "Why Some Merchants Accept Bitcoin Despite the Risks," *Payments Source*, May 21, 2013, http://www.paymentssource.com/news/why-some-merchants-accept-bitcoin-despite-the-risks-3014183-1.html.

41. Bailey Reutzel, "Some Risky Merchants Turn to Bitcoin Processor; Others Go It Alone," *Payments Source*, November 8, 2013, http://www.paymentssource.com/news/some-risky-merchants-turn-to-bitcoin-processor-others-go-it-alone-3015974-1.html.

42. Emily Maltby, "Chargebacks Create Business Headaches," *Wall Street Journal*, February 10, 2011, http://online.wsj.com/article/SB10001424052748704698004576104554234202010.html. One such scam involves Alice sending Bob a PayPal payment for a laptop that Bob has listed on Craigslist. Alice comes by Bob's house, picks up the laptop, and soon thereafter initiates a chargeback (i.e., reverses the payment). PayPal generally requires proof of shipment before reversing a chargeback, so Bob is out of luck.

43. Quoted in Rob Wile, "A Brooklyn Bodega Owner Told Us Why All Merchants Should Start Accepting Bitcoin," *Business Insider*, November 11, 2013, http://www.businessinsider.com/brooklyn-bitcoin-bodega-2013-11.

44. Dilip Ratha, et al., "Migration and Remittances: Recent Developments and Outlook" (Migration and Development Brief No. 25, World Bank, October 2015), http://pubdocs.worldbank.org/pubdocs/publicdoc/2015/10/102761445353157305/MigrationandDevelopmentBrief25.pdf.

45. Ibid.

46. Jessica Silver-Greenberg, "New Rules for Money Transfers, but Few Limits," *New York Times*, June 1, 2012, http://www.nytimes.com/2012/06/02/business/new-rules-for-money-transfers-but-few-limits.html?pagewanted=all&_r=0.

47. World Bank Payment Systems Development Group, *Remittance Prices Worldwide: An Analysis of Trends in the Average Total Cost of Migrant Remittance Services* (Washington, DC: World Bank, December 2015), https://remittanceprices.worldbank.org/sites/default/files/rpw_report_december_2015.pdf.

48. Kevin Watkins and Maria Quattri, *Lost in Intermediation: How Excessive Charges Undermine the Benefits of Remittances for Africa* (Overseas Development Institute Report, April 2014), http://www.odi.org/sites/odi.org.uk/files/odi-assets/publications-opinion-files/8901.pdf.

49. Grace Caffyn, "New Service Finds Optimum Bitcoin Transaction Fee," *CoinDesk*, July 28, 2015, http://www.coindesk.com/new-service-finds-optimum-bitcoin-transaction-fee/.

50. Tom Simonite, "Bitcoin Hits the Big Time, to the Regret of Some Early Boosters," *MIT Technology Review*, May 22, 2013, http://www.technologyreview.com/news/515061/bitcoin-hits-the-big-time-to-the-regret-of-some-early-boosters/.

51. Andrew R. Johnson, "Money Transfers in Bitcoins? Western Union, MoneyGram Weigh the Option," *Wall Street Journal*, April 18, 2013, http://online.wsj.com/article/SB10001424127887324493704578431000719258048.html.

52. Luis Buenaventura, "The Bootstrapper's Guide to Bitcoin Remittances," *TechCrunch*, January 30, 2015, http://techcrunch.com/2015/01/30/the-bootstrappers-guide-to-bitcoin-remittances/.

53. Daniel Cawrey, "Payments Veterans Seek to Unlock Blockchain's Power with Align Commerce," *CoinDesk*, January 11, 2015, http://www.coindesk.com/payments-veterans-seek-unlock-blockchains-power-align-commerce/.

54. Joon Ian Wong, "Bitspark Enters Hong Kong's Remittance Market with Bitcoin-Powered Solution," *CoinDesk*, November 25, 2014, http://www.coindesk.com/bitspark-hong-kong-remittance/.

55. Jon Southurst, "Philippines Startups Aim to Fulfil Bitcoin's Remittance Promise," *CoinDesk*, July 9, 2014, http://www.coindesk.com/philippines-startups-fulfil-bitcoins-remittance-promise/.

56. Joon Ian Wong, "Bitspark Rolls Out Remittance Service to Indonesia," *CoinDesk*, January 21, 2015, http://www.coindesk.com/bitspark-rolls-remittance-service-indonesia/.

57. Kadhim Shubber, "How BitPesa Plans to Reduce Friction in the Remittances Market," *CoinDesk*, June 16, 2014, http://www.coindesk.com/bitpesa-plans-reduce-friction-remittances-market/.

58. Muhammad Yunus, *Banker to the Poor: Micro-Lending and the Battle against World Poverty* (New York: Public Affairs, 2003).

59. Oya Pinar Ardic, Maximilien Heimann, and Nataliya Mylenko, "Access to Financial Services and the Financial Inclusion Agenda around the World" (Policy Research Working Paper 5537, World Bank Financial and Private Sector Development Consultative Group to Assist the Poor, January 2011), https://openknowledge.worldbank.org/bitstream/handle/10986/3310/WPS5537.pdf.

60. Jeff Fong, "How Bitcoin Could Help the World's Poorest People," *PolicyMic*, May 2013, http://mic.com/articles/41561/bitcoin-price-2013-how-bitcoin-could-help-the-world-s-poorest-people.

61. "Bitcoin Statistics," LocalBitcoins.com, accessed November 12, 2013, https://localbitcoins.com/statistics.

62. Vitalik Buterin, "Charity Focus: Sean's Outpost," *Bitcoin Magazine*, April 2013, http://bitcoinmagazine.com/sandbox/seansoutpost.pdf.

63. Ibid.

64. Vitalik Buterin, "Sean's Outpost Announces Satoshi Forest, Nine-Acre Sanctuary for the Homeless," *Bitcoin Magazine*, September 9, 2013, http://bitcoinmagazine.com/6939/seans-outpost-announces-satoshi-forest/; Pete Rizzo, "Community Rallies to Support Victims of Flooded

Satoshi Forest," *CoinDesk*, May 2, 2014, http://www.coindesk.com/community-rallies-support-victims-flooded-satoshi-forest/.

65. Meghan Lords, "Feeding and Housing the Homeless with Bitcoin," *Bitcoin Not Bombs*, August 16, 2013, http://www.bitcoinnotbombs.com/feeding-and-housing-the-homeless-with-bitcoin/.

66. Jon Matonis, "Bitcoin's Promise in Argentina," *Forbes*, April 27, 2013, http://www.forbes.com/sites/jonmatonis/2013/04/27/bitcoins-promise-in-argentina/.

67. Roberto A. Ferdman, "Argentina's Unofficial Consumer Confidence Metric Is Free-Falling Again," *Quartz*, October 23, 2013, http://qz.com/138498/argentinas-unofficial-consumer-confidence-metric-is-free-falling-again/.

68. Camila Russo, "Bitcoin Dreams Endure to Savers Crushed by CPI: Argentina Credit," *Bloomberg*, April 16, 2013, http://www.bloomberg.com/news/2013-04-16/bitcoin-dreams-endure-to-savers-crushed-by-cpi-argentina-credit.html.

69. Georgia Wells, "Bitcoin Downloads Surge in Argentina," *Money Beat, Wall Street Journal*, July 17, 2013, http://blogs.wsj.com/moneybeat/2013/07/17/bitcoin-downloads-surge-in-argentina/.

70. Ben Smith and Conz Preti, "Argentina's Net Party Is Ready for the Revolution," *BuzzFeed*, October 24, 2013, http://www.buzzfeed.com/bensmith/argentinas-net-party-is-ready-for-the-revolution.

71. Jerry Brito, "The Top 3 Things I Learned at the Bitcoin Conference," *Reason*, May 20, 2013, http://reason.com/archives/2013/05/20/the-top-3-things-i-learned-at-the-bitcoi.

72. Mike Hearn, "Bitcoin 2012 London: Mike Hearn," YouTube video, 28:19, posted by QueuePolitely, September 27, 2012, http://www.youtube.com/watch?v=mD4L7xDNCmA. Although smart property is still theoretical, the basic mechanisms are built into the Bitcoin protocol. See *Bitcoin wiki*, s.v. "Smart Property," accessed July 30, 2013, https://en.bitcoin.it/wiki/Smart_Property.

73. Houman Shadab, "What Are Smart Contracts, and What Can We Do with Them? A Backgrounder for Policymakers," *Coin Center*, December 15, 2014, http://coincenter.org/2014/12/smart-contracts/.

74. Rick Chen, "Pozible Now Accepting Pledges in Bitcoin," *Pozible*, October 25, 2013, http://www.pozible.com/blog/article/index/129.

75. Sandrine Ayral, "Bitcoin 2.0 Crowdfunding Is Real Crowdfunding," *TechCrunch*, October 17, 2014, http://techcrunch.com/2014/10/17/bitcoin-2-0-crowdfunding-is-real-crowdfunding/.

76. Stan Higgins, "Mike Hearn Wins $40k Bounty for Bitcoin Core Crowdfunding Platform," *CoinDesk*, July 2, 2014, http://www.coindesk.com/mike-hearn-wins-40000-bounty-bitcoin-core-crowdfunding/.

77. Jeff Yule, "Help Ronald McDonald House of Albany Buy a Medical Breast Pump," *Lightlist*, accessed April 20, 2015, https://www.lightlist.io/projects /help-ronald-mcdonald-house-of-albany-buy-a-medical-breast-pump#.

78. Wau Holland Stiftung, "GnuPG Donation," *Lightlist*, accessed April 20, 2015, https://www.lightlist.io/projects/gnupg-donation#.

79. Klint Finley, "Love Child of Bitcoin and GitHub Pays Cash for Code," *Wired*, December 17, 2013, http://www.wired.com/wiredenterprise/2013 /12/bithub/.

80. John Biggs, "Bitmonet Monetizes Your Blog through the Power of Bitcoin," *TechCrunch*, August 30, 2013, http://techcrunch.com/2013/08 /30/bitmonet-monetizes-your-blog-through-the-power-of-bitcoin/.

81. For more information about the following discussion, see Jerry Brito, Houman Shadab, and Andrea Castillo, "Bitcoin Financial Regulation: Securities, Derivatives, Prediction Markets, and Gambling," *Columbia Science and Technology Law Review* 16 (2014): 144–221.

82. *Securities and Exchange Commission v. Trendon T. Shavers and Bitcoin Savings and Trust*, Civil Action No. 4:13-CV-416 (E.D. Tex. 2014), http:// www.law.du.edu/documents/corporate-governance/securities-matters /shavers/SEC-v-Shavers-No-4-13-CV-416-E-D-Tex-Sept-18-2014.pdf.

83. Jon Matonis, "Bitcoin and iGaming: Disruption Comes from Your Blind Spot," *CoinDesk*, March 14, 2015, http://www.coindesk.com/bitcoin-and -igaming-disruption-comes-from-your-blind-spot/.

84. Robin Hanson, "Decision Markets," *IEEE Intelligent Systems* 14, no. 3 (May/June1999): 16–19.

85. Rachel Weiner, "Does Intrade Matter? Political Betting Explained," *Washington Post*, October 13, 2011, http://www.washingtonpost.com /blogs/the-fix/post/does-intrade-matter-political-betting-explained /2011/10/12/gIQAHqpdhL_blog.html.

86. US Commodity Futures Trading Commission, "CFTC Charges Ireland-Based 'Prediction Market' Proprietors Intrade and TEN with Violating the CFTC's Off-Exchange Options Trading Ban and Filing False Forms with the CFTC," November 26, 2012, http://www.cftc.gov/PressRoom /PressReleases/pr6423-12.

87. Jack Peterson and Joseph Krug, "Augur: a Decentralized, Open-Source Platform for Prediction Markets" (white paper, accessed April 20, 2015), http://www.augur.link/augur.pdf.

88. Andrea Castillo, "The Silk Road 2.0 Database Is Up for Grabs in the First Darkleaks Auction," *Ümlaut, Medium*, February 13, 2015, https://medium .com/the-umlaut/the-silk-road-2-0-database-is-up-for-grabs-in-the-first -darkleaks-auction-23ff0355cab0.

89. Lawrence H. White, "The Market for Cryptocurrencies" (GMU Working Paper in Economics No. 14-45, December 15, 2014), http://papers.ssrn .com/sol3/papers.cfm?abstract_id=2538290.

90. Morgan E. Peck, "The Bitcoin Arms Race Is On!" *IEEE Spectrum*, May 6, 2013, http://spectrum.ieee.org/computing/networks/the-bitcoin-arms-race-is-on.

91. Adam B. Levine, "Episode 71: Blockchain Tools and Litecoin Devs," (interview with Charlie Lee) *Let's Talk Bitcoin!*, December 31, 2013, https://letstalkbitcoin.com/e71-blockchain-tools-and-litecoin-devs/.

92. Eli Ben-Sasson et al., "Zerocash: Decentralized Anonymous Payments from Bitcoin," *Proceedings of the 2014 IEEE Symposium on Security and Privacy*, May 18, 2014, http://zerocash-project.org/media/pdf/zerocash-extended-20140518.pdf.

93. Even if Dogecoin did not make it "to the moon," its supporters take pride that it landed among the stars.

94. "Dogecoin to Sponsor Josh Wise Again at 'Dega" (staff report, May 22, 2014), NASCAR, http://www.nascar.com/en_us/news-media/articles/2014/5/22/josh-wise-dogecoin-sponsorship-talladega-sprint-fan-vote.html.

95. Danny Bradbury, "Colored Coins Paint Sophisticated Future for Bitcoin," *CoinDesk*, June 14, 2013, http://www.coindesk.com/colored-coins-paint-sophisticated-future-for-bitcoin/.

96. Sarah Todd, "Nasdaq Signals Confidence in Bitcoin, Not Just the Blockchain," *American Banker*, May 19, 2015, http://www.americanbanker.com/news/bank-technology/nasdaq-signals-confidence-in-bitcoin-not-just-the-blockchain-1074405-1.html.

97. Pete Rizzo, "Hands On With Linq, Nasdaq's Private Markets Blockchain Project," *CoinDesk*, November 21, 2015, http://www.coindesk.com/hands-on-with-linq-nasdaqs-private-markets-blockchain-project/.

98. Jeremy Kirk, "Could the Bitcoin Network Be Used as an Ultrasecure Notary Service?" *ComputerWorld*, May 23, 2013, http://www.computerworld.com/s/article/9239513/Could_the_Bitcoin_network_be_used_as_an_ultrasecure_notary_service_.

99. Named after cryptographer David Chaum who developed this technique, untraceable cash allows a sender to disguise the content of a message or transaction before it is signed. External parties can therefore verify the authenticity of that message or transaction without needing to view the contents. See David Chaum, "Blind Signatures for Untraceable Payments," *Advances in Cryptography* 82, no. 3 (1983): 199–203, http://www.hit.bme.hu/~buttyan/courses/BMEVIHIM219/2009/Chaum.BlindSigForPayment.1982.PDF.

100. Kyle Torpey, "Chris Odom Explains How Open Transactions Make Altcoins Irrelevant at Inside Bitcoins Conference," *CryptoCoinsNews*, September 21, 2014, https://www.cryptocoinsnews.com/chris-odom-explains-how-open-transactions-makes-altcoins-irrelevant-at-inside-bitcoins-conference/.

101. Jonathan Warren, "Bitmessage: A Peer-to-Peer Message Authentication and Delivery System" (white paper, November 27, 2012), https://bitmessage.org/bitmessage.pdf.

102. Eli Dourado, "Can Namecoin Obsolete ICANN (and More)?" *Ümlaut*, February 5, 2014, https://theumlaut.com/2014/02/05/namecoin-icann/.

103. The Namecoin project has struggled to maintain active users. A 2015 study of the ecosystem finds that only 28 of Namecoin's 120,000 registered domains are not squatted and host nontrivial content. No Namecoin addresses are known to have been traded. See Harry Kalodner, et al., "An Empirical Study of Namecoin and Lessons for Decentralized Namespace Design" (working paper presented to the 14th Annual Workshop on the Economics of Information Technology, June 22, 2015), http://www.econinfosec.org/archive/weis2015/papers/WEIS_2015_kalodner.pdf.

104. Daniel Cawrey, "BitPay Project Aims to Do for Networks What Bitcoin Did for Currency," *CoinDesk*, October 28, 2014, http://www.coindesk.com/bitpay-project-aims-networks-bitcoin-currency/.

105. Lefteris Karapetsas, "A Next-Generation Smart Contract and Decentralized Application Platform" (white paper), accessed January 28, 2016, https://github.com/ethereum/wiki/wiki/White-Paper.

106. J.R. Willett et al., "Omni Protocol Specification (formerly Mastercoin)" (white paper), accessed January 28, 2016, https://github.com/mastercoin-MSC/spec.

107. As of April 4, 2016, the market capitalization of Ethereum was around $890 million and the market capitalization of Ripple was roughly $258 million. All of the subsequent cryptocurrency comparisons were collected on April 4, 2016. See "Crypto-Currency Market Capitalizations," accessed April 4, 2016, http://coinmarketcap.com/.

108. Total reported venture capital in Bitcoin companies was $2 million in 2012, $95 million in 2013, $350 million in 2014, and $548.98 million in 2015, and roughly $500,000 in January of 2016, summing to a little over $1 billion in all-time overall investment. See "Bitcoin Venture Capital Investments," *CoinDesk*, accessed February 1, 2016, http://www.coindesk.com/bitcoin-venture-capital/.

109. Juniper Research reports that Bitcoin use far outstrips other altcoins, with 1.3 million active Bitcoin users in 2014. See Juniper Research, *The Future of Cryptocurrency: Bitcoin & Altcoins, Impact & Opportunities, 2015–2019*, February 2015, http://www.juniperresearch.com/researchstore/commerce-money/cryptocurrency/bitcoin-altcoin-impact-opportunities.

110. Bitcoin has roughly 31,000 total nodes and 4,500 active nodes while Litecoin has around 6,700 total nodes and 800 active nodes. See "Crypto-Currencies Statistics," BitInfoCharts, accessed February 1, 2016, https://bitinfocharts.com/.

111. Roughly 500,000 Bitcoin addresses are active, while Litecoin has around 11,000 active addresses. See ibid.

112. Bitcoin facilitates an average of around 9,000 transactions each hour at an average value of $8,200. Litecoin, in comparison, facilitates an average of roughly 250 transactions per hour at an average value of $2,000. See ibid.

113. Juniper Research, *The Future of Cryptocurrency*.

114. Adam Back et al., "Enabling Blockchain Innovations with Pegged Sidechains" (white paper, October 22, 2014), http://www.blockstream.com/sidechains.pdf.

115. Fred Wilson, "Sidechains," *AVC*, October 27, 2014, http://avc.com/2014/10/sidechains/.

116. Timothy B. Lee, "An Illustrated History of Bitcoin Crashes," *Forbes*, April 11, 2013, http://www.forbes.com/sites/timothylee/2013/04/11/an-illustrated-history-of-bitcoin-crashes/.

117. Felix Salmon, "The Bitcoin Bubble and the Future of Currency," *Medium*, April 3, 2013, https://medium.com/money-banking/2b5ef79482cb.

118. Maureen Farrell, "Strategist Predicts End of Bitcoin," *CNN Money*, May 14, 2013, http://money.cnn.com/2013/05/14/investing/bremmer-bitcoin/index.html.

119. Julia Schieffer, *The Virtual Frontier: Bitcoin Derivatives Are Coming!* (DerivSource report, November 2014), http://www.teraexchange.com/news/A-DerivSource-Special-Report-on-Bitcoin-Derivatives-Nov-2014.pdf.

120. Adam Gurri, "Bitcoins, Free Banking, and the Optional Clause," *Ümlaut*, May 6, 2013, http://theumlaut.com/2013/05/06/bitcoins-free-banking-and-the-optional-clause/.

121. Michael J. Casey, "TeraExchange Unveils First U.S.-Regulated Bitcoin Swaps Exchange," *Wall Street Journal*, September 12, 2014, http://www.wsj.com/articles/teraexchange-launches-bitcoin-derivatives-exchange-1410543989.

122. US Commodity Futures Trading Commission, "CFTC Requests Public Comment on Related Applications Submitted by LedgerX, LLC for Registration as a Derivatives Clearing Organization and Swap Execution Facility" (CFTC Press Release PR7078-14, December 15, 2014), http://www.cftc.gov/PressRoom/PressReleases/pr7078-14.

123. US Commodity Futures Trading Commission, "CFTC Issues Order of Temporary Registration as a Swap Execution Facility to LedgerX LLC" (CFTC Press Release PR7226-15, September 10, 2015), http://www.cftc.gov/PressRoom/PressReleases/pr7226-15.

124. Joon Ian Wong, "Ex-Goldman, Paribas Execs Launch Bitcoin Derivatives Exchange," *CoinDesk*, February 26, 2015, http://www.coindesk.com/former-goldman-director-launches-bitcoin-derivatives-exchange/.

125. Joon Ian Wong, "BitMEX to Launch Bitcoin 'Fear' Index," *CoinDesk*, December 31, 2014, http://www.coindesk.com/bitmex-launch-bitcoin-fear-index/.

126. Jerry Brito, "Why Bitcoin's Valuation Doesn't Really Matter," *Technology Liberation Front*, April 5, 2013, http://techliberation.com/2013/04/05/why-bitcoins-valuation-doesnt-really-matter/.

127. Today, merchant service providers accept the risk presented by the volatility and nevertheless maintain low fees. It remains to be seen whether this model will be sustainable in the long run.

128. Dan Kaminsky, "I Tried Hacking Bitcoin and I Failed," *Business Insider*, April 12, 2013, http://www.businessinsider.com/dan-kaminsky-highlights-flaws-bitcoin-2013-4.

129. Mitch Lipka, "Home Depot Hack Could Lead to $3 Billion in Fake Charges," *CBS News*, September 16, 2014, http://www.cbsnews.com/news/credit-monitoring-company-home-depot-breach-could-result-in-2b-in-fraud/.

130. Di Wang, "Secure Implementations of ECDSA Signatures in Bitcoin," ed. Nicholas T. Courtois (thesis for MSc in Information Security, University College London, September 17, 2014), http://www.nicolascourtois.com/bitcoin/thesis_Di_Wang.pdf.

131. Nicholas T. Courtois, Marek Grajek, and Rahul Naik, "Optimizing SHA256 in Bitcoin Mining," in *Communications in Computer and Information Science: Cryptography and Computer Systems* 448 (2014): 131–44.

132. Should hackers learn to crack SHA-256 or ECDSA, many more industries and technologies other than Bitcoin would be vulnerable to malicious attacks—including traditional financial institutions!

133. Kaminski, "I Tried Hacking Bitcoin."

134. Stephen Doherty, "All Your Bitcoins Are Ours . . ." *Security Response, Symantec*, June 16, 2011, http://www.symantec.com/connect/blogs/all-your-bitcoins-are-ours.

135. Devin Coldewey, "$250,000 Worth of Bitcoins Stolen in Net Heist," *NBC News*, September 5, 2012, http://www.nbcnews.com/technology/250-000-worth-bitcoins-stolen-net-heist-980871.

136. Zack Whittaker, "Bitstamp Exchange Hacked, $5M Worth of Bitcoin Stolen," *ZDNet*, January 5, 2015, http://www.zdnet.com/article/bitstamp-bitcoin-exchange-suspended-amid-hack-concerns-heres-what-we-know/.

137. Pete Rizzo, "Coinapult Claims $40k Lost in Hot Wallet Compromise," *CoinDesk*, March 17, 2015, http://www.coindesk.com/coinapult-loses-40k-hot-wallet-compromise/.

138. Jon Southurst, "'Good Samaritan' Blockchain Hacker Who Returned 267 BTC Speaks Out," *CoinDesk*, December 12, 2014, http://www.coindesk.com/good-samaritan-blockchain-hacker-returned-255-btc-speaks/.

139. Jon Southurst, "Hacker Returns 225 BTC Taken from Blockchain Wallets," *CoinDesk*, December 10, 2014, http://www.coindesk.com/hacker-returns-225-btc-taken-blockchain-wallets/.

140. Michael Carney, "Bitcoin Wallet Blockchain.info Accidentally Introduced a Software Vulnerability Last Night," *Pando*, December 8, 2014, http://pando.com/2014/12/08/bitcoin-wallet-blockchain-info-accidentally-introduced-a-software-vulnerability-last-night/.

141. Paul Vigna, "5 Things about Mt. Gox's Crisis," *Wall Street Journal*, February 25, 2014, http://blogs.wsj.com/briefly/2014/02/25/5-things-about-mt-goxs-crisis/.

142. Robert McMillan and Cade Metz, "The Rise and Fall of the World's Largest Bitcoin Exchange," *Wired*, November 6, 2013, http://www.wired.com/2013/11/mtgox/.

143. Yoshifumi Takemoto and Sophie Knight, "Mt. Gox Files for Bankruptcy, Hit with Lawsuit," *Reuters*, February 28, 2014, http://www.reuters.com/article/2014/02/28/us-bitcoin-mtgox-bankruptcy-idUSBREA1R0FX20140228.

144. Ben McLannahan, "Bitcoin Hack Report Suggests Inside Job," *Financial Times*, February 20, 2015, http://www.ft.com/intl/cms/s/0/b5538688-b853-11e4-a2fb-00144feab7de.html.

145. Michael J. de la Merced and Nathaniel Popper, "Trustee Moves to Repay Creditors in Mt. Gox Bitcoin Exchange," *DealBook*, *New York Times*, November 25, 2014, http://dealbook.nytimes.com/2014/11/25/mt-gox-bankruptcy-trustee-to-tap-kraken-exchange-in-repaying-creditors/.

146. Jon Russell, "Mt. Gox Customers Can Now File Claims for Their Lost Bitcoins," *TechCrunch*, April 22, 2015, http://techcrunch.com/2015/04/22/mt-gox-claims/.

147. Nermin Hajdarbegovic, "Coinbase Names Aon as Its Bitcoin Insurance Broker," *CoinDesk*, August 28, 2014, http://www.coindesk.com/coinbase-names-aon-bitcoin-insurance-broker/.

148. Michael J. Casey and Paul Vigna, "BitGo Adds Comprehensive Insurance to Its Services," *MoneyBeat*, *Wall Street Journal*, February 25, 2015, http://blogs.wsj.com/moneybeat/2015/02/25/bitbeat-bitgo-adds-comprehensive-insurance-to-its-services/.

149. Nermin Hajdarbegovic, "Kraken Bitcoin Exchange Passes 'Proof of Reserves' Cryptographic Audit," *CoinDesk*, March 24, 2014, http://www.coindesk.com/krakens-audit-proves-holds-100-bitcoins-reserve/.

150. *Wikipedia*, s.v. "Deep Web," accessed July 30, 2013, http://en.wlkıpedia.org/wiki/Deep_Web.

151. NiLolas Christin, *Traveling the Silk Road: A Measurement Analysis of a Large Anonymous Online Marketplace* (Carnegie Mellon CyLab Technical Report CMU-CyLab-12-018, July 30, 2012, revised November 28, 2012), http://www.cylab.cmu.edu/files/pdfs/tech_reports/CMUCyLab12018.pdf.

152. Jerry Brito, "*National Review* Gets Bitcoin Very Wrong," *Technology Liberation Front*, June 20, 2013, http://techliberation.com/2013/06/20/national-review-gets-bitcoin-very-wrong/.

153. Adrian Chen, "The Underground Website Where You Can Buy Any Drug Imaginable," *Gawker*, June 1, 2011, http://gawker.com/5805928/the-underground-website-where-you-can-buy-any-drug-imaginable.

154. Brett Wolf, "Senators Seek Crackdown on 'Bitcoin' Currency," *Reuters*, June 8, 2011, http://www.reuters.com/article/2011/06/08/us-financial-bitcoins-idUSTRE7573T320110608.

155. Emily Flitter, "FBI Shuts Alleged Online Drug Marketplace, Silk Road," *Reuters*, October 2, 2013, http://www.reuters.com/article/2013/10/02/us-crime-silkroad-raid-idUSBRE9910TR20131002.

156. James Ball, Charles Arthur, and Adam Gabbatt, "FBI Claims Largest Bitcoin Seizure after Arrest of Alleged Silk Road Founder," *Bitcoin*, *Guardian*, October 2, 2013, http://www.theguardian.com/technology/2013/oct/02/alleged-silk-road-website-founder-arrested-bitcoin.

157. Brian Krebs, "Feds Arrest Alleged Top Silk Road Drug Dealer," *Krebs on Security*, October 7, 2013, http://krebsonsecurity.com/2013/10/feds-arrest-alleged-top-silk-road-drug-seller/.

158. Ryan Mac, "False Alarm: Silk Road Competitor Black Market Reloaded Staying Online," *Forbes*, October 18, 2013, http://www.forbes.com/sites/ryanmac/2013/10/18/false-alarm-silk-road-competitor-black-market-reloaded-staying-online/.

159. Leonid Bershidsky, "Goodbye Silk Road, Hello Sheep Marketplace," *Bloomberg*, October 4, 2013, http://www.bloomberg.com/news/2013-10-04/goodbye-silk-road-hello-sheep-marketplace.html.

160. Andy Greenberg, "'Silk Road 2.0' Launches, Promising a Resurrected Black Market for the Dark Web," *Forbes*, November 6, 2013, http://www.forbes.com/sites/andygreenberg/2013/11/06/silk-road-2-0-launches-promising-a-resurrected-black-market-for-the-dark-web/.

161. Gwern, "2014 in the Dark Net Markets: By the Numbers," *Deep.Dot.Web*, January 3, 2015, http://www.deepdotweb.com/2015/01/03/2014-in-the-dark-net-markets-by-the-numbers/.

162. Andy Greenberg, "Silk Road Competitor Shuts Down and Another Plans to Go Offline after Claimed $6 Million Theft," *Forbes*, December 1, 2013, http://www.forbes.com/sites/andygreenberg/2013/12/01/silk-road-competitor-shuts-down-and-another-plans-to-go-offline-after-6-million-theft/.

163. Brian Krebs, "Feds Arrest Alleged 'Silk Road 2' Admin, Seize Servers," *Krebs on Security*, November 6, 2014, http://krebsonsecurity.com/2014/11/feds-arrest-alleged-silk-road-2-admin-seize-servers/.

164. Statistics from DarkNet Stats, accessed January 28, 2016, https://dnstats.net/#.

165. Andy Greenberg, "Creators of New Fed-Proof Bitcoin Marketplace Swear It's Not for Drugs," *Wired*, August 28, 2014, http://www.wired.com/2014/08/openbazaar-not-for-drugs/.
166. "Liberty Reserve Digital Money Service Forced Offline," *BBC News*, May 27, 2013, http://www.bbc.co.uk/news/technology-22680297.
167. Jeffrey Sparshott, "Bitcoin Exchange Makes Apparent Move to Play by U.S. Money-Laundering Rules," *Wall Street Journal*, June 28, 2013, http://online.wsj.com/article/SB10001424127887323873904578574000957464468.html.
168. Sam Rozenfeld, "FCC's VoIP Regulation Dilemma," *Telephony Your Way*, April 30, 2011, http://www.telephonyyourway.com/2011/04/30/fccs-voip-regulation-dilemma/.
169. U.S. Const. art I § 10.
170. Reuben Grinberg, "Bitcoin: An Innovative Alternative Digital Currency," *Hastings Science & Technology Law Journal* 4 (2011): 159–208.
171. Blake Ellis, "Local Currencies: 'In the U.S. We Don't Trust,'" *CNN Money*, January 27, 2012, http://money.cnn.com/2012/01/17/pf/local_currency/index.htm.
172. 18 U.S.C. §§ 485 and 486.
173. Grinberg, "Bitcoin," 193n158.
174. *Hearing on the Regulation of Non-bank Money Transmitter—Money Services Businesses*, 112th Congress (2012), statement of Ezra C. Levine on behalf of the Money Services Round Table before the Subcommittee on Financial Institutions and Consumer Credit of the House Committee on Financial Services, http://financialservices.house.gov/uploadedfiles/hhrg-112-ba15-wstate-elevine-20120621.pdf.
175. US Department of Treasury, Financial Crimes Enforcement Network, "Application of FinCEN's Regulations to Persons Administering, Exchanging, or Using Virtual Currencies" (Guidance FIN-2013-G001, March 18, 2013), http://www.fincen.gov/statutes_regs/guidance/html/FIN-2013-G001.html.
176. 18 U.S.C. § 1960.
177. Aaron Greenspan, *Held Hostage: How the Banking Sector Has Distorted Financial Regulation and Destroyed Technological Progress* (Palo Alto, CA: Think Computer Corporation, 2011), http://works.bepress.com/aaron_greenspan/1/.
178. Ibid., 3.
179. 31 U.S.C. § 5311.
180. US Department of Treasury, Financial Crimes Enforcement Network, "Application of FinCEN's Regulations to Persons Administering, Exchanging, or Using Virtual Currencies" (Guidance FIN-2013-G001,

March 18, 2013), http://www.fincen.gov/statutes_regs/guidance/html/FIN-2013-G001.html.

181. See 31 CFR § 1010.100(ff)(5)(ii)(A)–(F).

182. For example, US Department of the Treasury, Financial Crimes and Enforcement Network, "Application of FinCEN's Regulations to Virtual Currency Mining Operations" (FIN-2014-R001, January 30, 2014), http://www.fincen.gov/news_room/rp/rulings/pdf/FIN-2014-R001.pdf; "Application of FinCEN's Regulations to Virtual Currency Software Development and Certain Investment Activity" (FIN-2014-R002, January 30, 2014), http://www.fincen.gov/news_room/rp/rulings/pdf/FIN-2014-R002.pdf; "Application of Money Services Business Regulations to the Rental of Computer Systems for Mining Virtual Currency" (FIN-2014-R007, April 29, 2014), http://www.fincen.gov/news_room/rp/rulings/pdf/FIN-2014-R007.pdf; "Request for Administrative Ruling on the Application of FinCEN's Regulations to a Virtual Currency Trading Platform" (FIN-2014-R011, October 27, 2014), http://www.fincen.gov/news_room/rp/rulings/pdf/FIN-2014-R011.pdf; "Request for Administrative Ruling on the Application of FinCEN's Regulations to a Virtual Currency Payment System" (FIN-2014-R012, October 27, 2014), http://www.fincen.gov/news_room/rp/rulings/pdf/FIN-2014-R012.pdf.

183. Tony Gallippi, "How FinCEN Guidelines Affect BitPay," *BitPay* blog, March 23, 2013, https://blog.bitpay.com/how-fincen-guidelines-affect-bitpay/.

184. US Department of the Treasury, Financial Crimes and Enforcement Network, "Request for Administrative Ruling on the Application of FinCEN's Regulations to Virtual Currency Mining Operations" (FIN-2014-R011, October 27, 2014), http://www.fincen.gov/news_room/rp/rulings/pdf/FIN-2014-R011.pdf.

185. Pete Rizzo, "FinCEN Rules Bitcoin Payment Processors, Exchanges are Money Transmitters," *CoinDesk*, October 27, 2014, http://www.coindesk.com/fincen-rules-bitcoin-payment-processors-exchanges-money-transmitters/.

186. US Department of the Treasury, Financial Crimes Enforcement Network, "Application of FinCEN's Regulations to Virtual Currency Mining Operations" (FIN-2014-R001, January 30, 2014), http://www.fincen.gov/news_room/rp/rulings/pdf/FIN-2014-R001.pdf.

187. Ibid.

188. Ibid.

189. Ibid.

190. Ibid.

191. South Carolina and Montana do not require money-transmission licensure.

192. Thomas Brown, "50-STATE SURVEY: Money Transmitter Licensing Requirements," http://abnk.assembly.ca.gov/sites/abnk.assembly.ca.gov

/files/50%20State%20Survey%20-%20MTL%20Licensing %20Requirements%2872986803_4%29.pdf.

193. David Landsman, "Government Oversight of Non-Bank Financial Institutions in the United States: Why Change Is Urgently Needed" (white paper, National Money Transmitters Association, September 12, 2012), http://www.paymentlawadvisor.com/files/2011/09/Government-Oversight-of-Non-Bank-Financial-institutions-NMTA.pdf.

194. Baily Reutzel, "In Money Transmitter Licensing, Is It Better to Own—or to Rent?" *Payments Source*, August 22, 2013, http://www.paymentssource.com/news/in-money-transmitter-licensing-is-it-better-to-own-or-to-rent-3015198-1.html.

195. Adam Thierer, *Permissionless Innovation: The Continuing Case for Comprehensive Technological Freedom* (Arlington, VA: Mercatus Center at George Mason University, 2014).

196. Jerry Brito, "US Regulations Are Hampering Bitcoin's Growth," *Bitcoin, Guardian*, November 18, 2013, http://www.theguardian.com/commentisfree/2013/nov/18/bitcoin-senate-hearings-regulation.

197. Marco Santori, "What Is Money Transmission and Why Does It Matter? A Backgrounder for Policymakers," *Coin Center*, April 7, 2015, https://coincenter.org/2015/04/what-is-money-transmission-and-why-does-it-matter/.

198. Shirley Siluk, "Virginia Compliance Issue Leads FastCash4Bitcoins to Suspend Service," *CoinDesk*, June 3, 2013, http://www.coindesk.com/virginia-compliance-issue-leads-fastcash4bitcoins-to-suspend-service/.

199. Michael del Castillo, "Fred Wilson: Oppressive Bitcoin Regulation Could Make Silicon Valley the 'Next Wall Street,'" *New York Business Journal*, April 24, 2015, http://www.bizjournals.com/newyork/news/2015/04/24/fred-wilson-silicon-valley-next-wall-street.html.

200. Jess Davis, "Texas Bank Regulator Says Bitcoin Exchanges Need Licenses," *Law360*, April 4, 2014, http://www.law360.com/articles/525406/texas-bank-regulator-says-bitcoin-exchanges-need-licenses.

201. Greg Farrell, "N.Y. Subpoenas Bitcoin Firms in Probe on Criminal Risk," *Bloomberg*, August 12, 2013, http://www.bloomberg.com/news/articles/2013-08-12/n-y-regulator-subpoenas-firms-over-bitcoin-crime-risks.

202. New York Department of Financial Services, "Public Hearing Regarding Virtual Currencies," January 28–29, 2014, http://www.dfs.ny.gov/about/hearings/vc_01282014_indx.htm.

203. 23 NY C.R.R. 200, http://www.dfs.ny.gov/legal/regulations/adoptions/dfsp200t.pdf.

204. Ben Lawsky, "As Requested, I'm Ben Lawsky, Superintendent of the NY Dept of Financial Services, Here for an AMA on Bitcoin/Virtual Currency," Reddit, February 20, 2014, http://www.reddit.com/r/IAmA/comments/1ygcil/as_requested_im_ben_lawsky_superintendent_of_the.

205. Matt Anderson, "NY DFS Releases Proposed BitLicense Regulatory Framework for Virtual Currency Firms," New York Department of Financial Services, July 17, 2014, http://www.dfs.ny.gov/about/press/pr1407171.htm.

206. Jerry Brito and Eli Dourado, "Comments to the New York Department of Financial Services on the Proposed Virtual Currency Regulatory Framework" (Public Interest Comment, Mercatus Center at George Mason University, Arlington, VA, August 14, 2014), http://mercatus.org/sites/default/files/BritoDourado-NY-Virtual-Currency-comment-081414.pdf.

207. New York Department of Financial Services, "Comments Regarding the Proposed Virtual Currency Regulatory Framework," http://www.dfs.ny.gov/legal/vcrf_comments.htm.

208. New York State Department of Financial Services, *New York Codes, Rules and Regulations*, http://www.dfs.ny.gov/legal/regulations/adoptions/dfsp200t.pdf.

209. Peter Van Valkenburgh and Jerry Brito, "Comments to the New York Department of Financial Services on the Revised Virtual Currency Regulatory Framework," *Coin Center*, March 27, 2015, http://coincenter.org/wp-content/uploads/2015/03/Coin-Center-BitLicense-Comment-March-2015.pdf.

210. Daniel Roberts, "Behind the 'Exodus' of Bitcoin Startups from New York," *Fortune*, August 14, 2015, http://fortune.com/2015/08/14/bitcoin-startups-leave-new-york-bitlicense/.

211. Yessi Bello Perez, "The Real Cost of Applying for a New York BitLicense," *CoinDesk*, August 13, 2015, http://www.coindesk.com/real-cost-applying-new-york-bitlicense/.

212. Daniel Roberts, "Bitcoin Company Ditches New York, Blaming New Regulations," *Fortune*, June 11, 2015, http://fortune.com/2015/06/11/bitcoin-shapeshift-new-york-bitlicense/.

213. A.B. 1326, 2015–16 Session (Cal. 2015).

214. Conference of State Bank Supervisors, "State Regulatory Requirements for Virtual Currency Activities: CSBS Model Regulatory Framework," September 15, 2015, https://www.csbs.org/regulatory/ep/Documents/CSBS-Model-Regulatory-Framework(September%2015%202015).pdf.

215. Peter Van Valkenburgh, "Freshly Unveiled CSBS Model Regs: Good Goals, Poor Execution," *Coin Center*, September 15, 2015, https://coincenter.org/2015/09/freshly-unveiled-csbs-model-regs-good-goals-poor-execution/.

216. Judith Rinearson, "Easier Transmitter Partnerships Should Be Encouraged, Not Hindered," *Payments Source*, December 18, 2014, http://www.paymentssource.com/news/interchange/easier-transmitter-partnerships-should-be-encouraged-not-hindered-3019986-1.html.

217. Bailey Reutzel, "Uniform Licensing Could Help Bitcoin Businesses Stay Disruptive," *Payments Source*, June 19, 2013, http://www.paymentssource.com/news/uniform-licensing-could-help-bitcoin-businesses-stay-disruptive-3014466-1.html.

218. IRS, "IRS Virtual Currency Guidance," Notice 2014-21, April 14, 2014, http://www.irs.gov/irb/2014-16_IRB/ar12.html.

219. James R. White, "Virtual Economies and Currencies: Additional IRS Guidance Could Reduce Tax Compliance Risks," Government Accountability Office, GAO-13-516, May 2013, http://www.gao.gov/assets/660/654620.pdf.

220. IRS, "IRS Virtual Currency Guidance," Notice 2014-21, April 14, 2014, http://www.irs.gov/irb/2014-16_IRB/ar12.html.

221. Department of the Treasury, Reports Relating to Currency in Excess of $10,000 Received as Bail by Court Clerks, C.F.R. 1010.331.

222. "How Do I Report Taxes?" *Coinbase*, October 1, 2014, https://support.coinbase.com/customer/portal/articles/1496488-how-do-i-report-taxes-.

223. George Selgin, "Synthetic Commodity Money" (working paper, Department of Economics, University of Georgia, Athens, 2013), http://papers.ssrn.com/sol3/papers.cfm?abstract_id=2000118.

224. 7 U.S.C. § 2(C) and 2(E).

225. 7 U.S.C. § 1a (9).

226. Massad, Testimony before the Senate Committee on Agriculture, Nutrition, and Forestry, December 10, 2014, http://www.cftc.gov/PressRoom/SpeechesTestimony/opamassad-6.

227. Ibid.

228. Mark Wetjen, "Bringing Commodities Regulation to Bitcoin," *Wall Street Journal*, November 3, 2014, http://www.wsj.com/articles/mark-wetjen-bringing-commodities-regulation-to-bitcoin-1415060058.

229. US Commodity Futures Trading Commission, "Special Address of CFTC Commissioner J. Christopher Giancarlo Before the Depository Trust & Clearing Corporation 2016 Blockchain Symposium," March 29, 2016, http://www.cftc.gov/PressRoom/SpeechesTestimony/opagiancarlo-13.

230. US Commodity Futures Trading Commission, "CFTC Issues Notice of Temporary Registration as a Swap Execution Facility to TeraExchange, LLC," September 19, 2013, http://www.cftc.gov/PressRoom/PressReleases/pr6698-13.

231. Latham & Watkins, "GMAC/CFTC Hosts Open Meeting Regarding Bitcoin and Digital Currency" (Client Alert Commentary No. 1757, October 21, 2014).

232. Stan Higgins, "TeraExchange Receives US Approval to Launch First Bitcoin Derivative," *CoinDesk*, September 12, 2014, http://www.coindesk.com/teraexchange-bitcoin-derivative-cftc/.

233. US Commodity Futures Trading Commission, "CFTC Orders Bitcoin Options Trading Platform Operator and Its CEO to Cease Illegally Offering Bitcoin Options and to Cease Operating a Facility for Trading or Processing of Swaps without Registering," September 17, 2015, http://www.cftc.gov/PressRoom/PressReleases/pr7231-15.

234. Michael J. Casey, "CFTC Commissioner Says Agency Has Authority over Bitcoin Price Manipulation," *Wall Street Journal*, November 17, 2014, http://www.wsj.com/articles/cftc-commissioner-says-agency-has-authority-over-bitcoin-price-manipulation-1416265016.

235. US Commodity Futures Trading Commission, Prohibition Against Manipulation, 17 C.F.R. § 180.

236. Aruna Viswanatha and Jacob Bunge, "CFTC Sues Kraft, Mondelez for Alleged Manipulation of Wheat Market," *Wall Street Journal*, April 1, 2015, http://www.wsj.com/articles/kraft-mondelez-sued-by-cftc-for-alleged-manipulation-of-wheat-market-1427929832.

237. Jared Paul Marx, "The Future of a Commodity: Bitcoin Regulation and the CFTC," *CoinDesk*, December 10, 2014, http://www.coindesk.com/future-commodity-bitcoin-regulation-cftc/.

238. Brito, Shadab, and Castillo, "Bitcoin Financial Regulation."

239. "Frequently Asked Questions," DEMO Trading Corp., accessed February 1, 2016.

240. EC Office of Investor Education and Advocacy, "Ponzi Schemes Using Virtual Currencies" (Investor Alert, July 23, 2013), http://investor.gov/sites/default/files/ia_virtualcurrencies.pdf.

241. Ibid.

242. Sec. & Exch. Comm'n v. Shavers, No. 4:13-CV-416, 2013 WL 4028182 at *1 (E.D. Tex. Aug. 6, 2013).

243. Vitalik Buterin, "The Pirate Saga: And So It Ends," *Bitcoin Magazine*, August 30, 2012, http://bitcoinmagazine.com/2126/the-pirate-saga-and-so-it-ends/.

244. Sec. & Exch. Comm'n v. Shavers, No. 4:13-CV-416, 2013 WL 4028182 at *1 (E.D. Tex. Aug. 6, 2013).

245. Edward V. Murphy, M. Maureen Murphy, and Michael V. Seitzinger, *Bitcoin: Questions, Answers, and Analysis of Legal Issues* (Congressional Research Service Report No. 7-5700, October 13, 2015), http://www.fas.org/sgp/crs/misc/R43339.pdf.

246. Securities and Exchange Commission, "SEC Sanctions Operator of Bitcoin-Related Stock Exchange for Registration Violations," December 8, 2014, http://www.sec.gov/News/PressRelease/Detail/PressRelease/1370543655716#.VSPyCPnF8Ro.

247. Jonathan Stacke, "Bitcoin Securities Exchange BTC-TC Shutters $12M Operations, Cites Regulatory Environment," *Genesis Block*, September 23, 2013, http://www.thebitcoinchannel.com/archives/23739.

248. Securities and Exchange Commission, Registration Statement: Winklevoss Bitcoin Trust, July 1, 2013, http://www.sec.gov/Archives/edgar/data/1579346/000119312513279830/d562329ds1.htm.
249. Yessi Bello Perez, "Bitcoin Investment Trust Gets FINRA Green Light to Trade," *CoinDesk*, March 2, 2015, http://www.coindesk.com/bitcoin-investment-trust-gets-finra-green-light-to-trade/.
250. Jason Somensatto, "How are Cryptocurrency Investments Different Than Securities Investments?" *Coin Center*, February 11, 2015, http://coincenter.org/2015/02/cryptocurrency-investments-different-securities-investments/.
251. Kashmir Hill, "The First 'Bitcoin 2.0' Crowd Sale Was a Wildly Successful $7 Million Disaster," *Forbes*, June 3, 2014, http://www.forbes.com/sites/kashmirhill/2014/06/03/mastercoin-maidsafe-crowdsale/.
252. Vitalik Buterin, "Launching the Ether Sale," *Ethereum*, July 22, 2014, https://blog.ethereum.org/2014/07/22/launching-the-ether-sale/.
253. Securities and Exchange Commission v. W. J. Howey Co., 328 U.S. 293 (1946).
254. See Peter Van Valkenburgh, "Framework for Securities Regulation of Cryptocurrencies," January 25, 2016, https://coincenter.org/2016/01/securities-framework/.
255. Ibid.
256. CFPB, "Risks to Consumers."
257. 15 U.S.C. §§ 1601–1692 (2013).
258. Board of Governors of the Federal Reserve System, Electronic Fund Transfers, 12 C.F.R. §§ 205.1–205.20.
259. 15 U.S.C. § 1693(b).
260. Consumer Financial Protection Bureau, CFPB Notice of Proposed Rulemaking, Prepaid Accounts Under the Electronic Fund Transfer Act (Regulation E) and the Truth in Lending Act (Regulation Z), (December 23, 2015) available at https://www.federalregister.gov/articles/2014/12/23/2014-27286/prepaid-accounts-under-the-electronic-fund-transfer-act-regulation-e-and-the-truth-in-lending-act.
261. 15 U.S.C. § 1693a (7).
262. 15 U.S.C. § 1693a (9).
263. Matthew Sparkes, "Winklevoss Twins Back Bitcoin as Bubble Bursts," *Telegraph*, April 12, 2013, http://www.telegraph.co.uk/technology/news/9989610/Winklevoss-twins-back-bitcoin-as-bubble-bursts.html.
264. *Bitcoin wiki*, s.v. "Browser-based wallet," accessed January 28, 2016, https://en.bitcoin.it/wiki/EWallet.
265. Consumer Financial Protection Bureau, "Summary of the Final Remittance Transfer Rule (Amendment to Regulation E)," 2013, http://

www.consumerfinance.gov/remittances-transfer-rule-amendment-to-regulation-e/#summary.

266. Ibid.

267. Multisignature transactions, wherein bitcoins cannot be transmitted until a predetermined number of multiple private keys sign it, allow more reversibility than standard single-key bitcoin transactions.

268. Andy Greenberg, "Founder of Drug Site Silk Road Says Bitcoin Booms and Busts Won't Kill His Black Market," *Forbes*, April 16, 2013, http://www.forbes.com/sites/andygreenberg/2013/04/16/founder-of-drug-site-silk-road-says-bitcoin-booms-and-busts-wont-kill-his-black-market/.

269. Senators Charles Schumer and Joe Manchin to Attorney General Eric Holder and Drug Enforcement Administration Administrator Michele Leonhart, June 6, 2011, http://www.manchin.senate.gov/public/index.cfm/press-releases?ID=284ae54a-acf1-4258-be1c-7acee1f7e8b3.

270. Jan Jahosky, "BitPay Eclipses Silk Road in Bitcoin Sales with Explosive $5.2M March," *Reuters*, April 2, 2013, http://www.reuters.com/article/ga-bitpay-idUSnBwZJkGla+b4+BSW20130402.

271. Matt Clinch, "Bitcoin Utopia? Interest Is Sky High in This Euro Nation," *CNBC*, April 5, 2013, http://www.cnbc.com/id/100618694.

272. Jan Jahosky, "BitPay Exceeds 1,000 Merchants Accepting Bitcoin," *Business Wire*, September 11, 2012, http://www.businesswire.com/news/home/20120911005855/en/BitPay-Exceeds-1000-Merchants-Accepting-Bitcoin.

273. See, for example: Jerry Brito and Peter Van Valkenburgh, "State Digital Currency Principles and Framework" (Coin Center Report, Coin Center, April 2015), https://coincenter.org/2015/04/state-digital-currency-principles-and-framework/.

274. Conference of State Bank Supervisors, "State Regulatory Requirements for Virtual Currency Activities, CSBS Draft Model Regulatory Framework and Request for Public Comment," December 16, 2014, http://www.csbs.org/regulatory/ep/Documents/CSBS%20Draft%20Model%20Regulatory%20Framework%20for%20Virtual%20Currency%20Proposal%20--%20Dec.%2016%202014.pdf.

ABOUT THE AUTHORS

Jerry Brito is the executive director of Coin Center, a nonprofit research and advocacy center focused on the public policy issues facing cryptocurrency technologies such as Bitcoin. He also serves as an adjunct professor of law at George Mason University. He is the coauthor of *Bitcoin: A Primer for Policymakers*, as well as other scholarly works on the regulation of cryptocurrencies. Brito has over ten years' experience in technology policy, and he has testified twice before Congress on cryptocurrencies. His op-eds have appeared in the *Wall Street Journal*, the *New York Times*, and elsewhere. Brito is a coauthor, with Susan Dudley, of *Regulation: A Primer*, and the editor of *Copyright Unbalanced: From Incentive to Excess*. He hosted *Surprisingly Free*, a weekly half-hour podcast featuring in-depth discussions with an eclectic mix of authors, academics, and entrepreneurs at the intersection of technology, policy, and economics. He also contributes to the *Technology Liberation Front*, a leading technology-policy blog. He has created several websites to foster transparency and accountability in government, including OpenRegs.com, which provides an alternative interface to the federal government's regulatory docketing system. Brito received his JD from George Mason University School of Law and his BA in political science from Florida International University.

Andrea Castillo is the program manager of the Technology Policy Program for the Mercatus Center at George Mason University. Her research focuses on technology policy, cybersecurity, cryptocurrency, and online speech. Castillo writes a bimonthly column for *Reason* covering the intersection of technology, economics, policy, and culture. She is a coauthor of *Bitcoin: A Primer for Policymakers* with Jerry Brito and *Liberalism and Cronyism: Two Rival Political and Economic Systems* with Randall G. Holcombe. Castillo is pursuing her PhD in economics at George Mason University and received her BS in economics and political science from Florida State University.

INDEX

Page numbers in *italics* indicate figures.

Made in the USA
Las Vegas, NV
07 February 2022

43407836R00066